A LEAP ACROSS THE ATLANTIC

THE MEMOIRS OF TWO BALLET DANCERS

By Christine Du Boulay Ellis

Edited by Lucia Mauro

Published by
Gorski Advertising – Hillside, IL
2006

Library of Congress Catalog Card Number TXU1-252-442

To Richard—the other ballet dancer, my love and partner in life.

From "The Fiddler of Dooney"

For the good are always merry,
Save by some evil chance,
And the merry love the fiddle,
And the merry love to dance.

— William Butler Yeats

THE MEMOIRS OF
TWO BALLET DANCERS

BY

CHRISTINE DU BOULAY ELLIS

Contents

Foreword

This book is about two talented English ballet dancers, whom I have known since we shared the stage as youngsters. It starts in England at the resurgence of ballet there, and travels to the world of dance in America today. Through the journey we meet famous, important people in the arts—dancers, choreographers, musicians, and painters they have known. Above all, we see how their love of and devotion to the art of ballet manifests itself in the pages of this beautiful book, enriching their lives and ours. A treasure!

Frederic Franklin CBE

Preface

The place was the Royal Opera House London. The date was February 20th, 1996, the 50th anniversary of the re-opening of the famous theatre after World War II, during which time it had been used as a dance hall. My husband Richard and I had been invited by Sir Anthony Dowell to be part of the occasion, which was to be celebrated with a performance of *The Sleeping Beauty* by the Royal Ballet.

Richard and I were sitting with the audience on the main floor. There was a stir, and we all rose as Her Majesty Queen Elizabeth entered the Royal Box. The orchestra began to play "God Save the Queen." The whole scene was overwhelming. After the National Anthem we sat, and the orchestra started the familiar strains of *The Sleeping Beauty*, which Richard and I had appeared in 50 years before.

I thought, how did we arrive at this exciting and momentous event? It brought back so many memories. I wondered if someday I should try and record them. But because dance and painting have been my best-known forms of expression, I was hesitant as a novice writer about writing our memoirs. But at the urging of many friends, I decided to go ahead and write down some of the events, places and people that have affected our lives.

Prologue

Our memoirs begin with Richard's birth in London, to his becoming a child actor and dancer, to his joining the Vic-Wells Ballet (Sadler's Wells Ballet) for its third season in 1933, where he stayed creating roles in the ever-increasing repertoire of the young company, under the direction of the brave and determined Ninette de Valois.

During this time, Richard was closely associated with emerging stars of the ballet world: Margot Fonteyn, Robert Helpmann, Frederick Ashton, Frederic Franklin and others.

Richard was also with the company on its ill-fated tour of Holland when it narrowly escaped the German army's invasion in 1940.

Then at the outset of England's war with Germany, Richard enlisted in the Royal Navy, thus interrupting his ballet career for more than five years. During this time he was on a considerable amount of active duty, including the D-Day assault on Omaha Beach, followed by more active duty in Holland. At the end of the war, he returned to the Sadler's Wells Ballet in time for its first performance at the Royal Opera House, where he met me as I was joining the company for the first time.

I was born and bred in Ealing, a western suburb of London. My father was English and in the Royal Air Force. My mother was Irish and born in Dublin. After their early separation, I lived with my mother in Ealing, where I gradually became involved in ballet, first at my academic school and then at the Sadler's Wells Ballet School. At that time, I was also attending art classes at the Central School of Art in Holborn, London.

When World War II started, my mother and I were on holiday in Ireland. At Miss de Valois' recommendation, we remained in Dublin so that I could study ballet with a teacher she knew there who had a ballet school and small performing group. With this group, I danced in operas, individual productions and in plays at the famous Gate Theatre.

Returning to London and to the Sadler's Wells Ballet School in 1942, I soon joined the International Ballet, where I stayed for three years until the end of the war, at which time I joined the Sadler's Wells Ballet for the season at Covent Garden, where I met Richard.

The memoirs continue with the events of our lives together. We were married the year after meeting and were together on tours of Europe and the first significant tours to the United States and Canada in 1949 and 1950.

Then Richard's previous back injury resulted in his having to give up performing. So we sought an answer to our future. It came in the form of an invitation to open a ballet school in Chicago. We took the offer and made the leap across the Atlantic, leaving our homeland to live in America—a hard decision, but one we have never regretted.

Our early days in Chicago were difficult, mainly due to lack of money and increasing problems with our sponsor. Matters came to a head, which led to our decision to open the Ellis-Du Boulay School of Ballet in 1954.

Things looked up. We had talented students, some with potential as choreographers, leading to the establishment of the Illinois Ballet in 1959. We directed the company for 12 years, fulfilling our wish to promote local talent. We produced many original ballets, with original sets and costumes. We performed throughout Chicago and neighboring states, and appeared many times on Channel 11-WTTW, Chicago's Public Broadcasting Station.

In 1970, Ruth Page invited Richard to replace Anton Dolin as Herr Drosselmeyer in her long-running production of *The Nutcracker*.

We continued teaching and coaching until 1994, when we closed our school after 40 years.

During the last years, I returned to painting and exhibited my watercolors.

We have been fortunate to know many ballet luminaries from our days in England and in America. We have had connections with teachers and teaching organizations in Illinois and other states, and we have staged ballets for companies both large and small.

All of these people and events have helped to make ours an interesting and rewarding life.

Acknowledgements

I offer my special thanks to Frederic Franklin for so graciously writing the Foreword to these memoirs.

And also my deep gratitude to Audre Deckmann Mendel for her help and encouragement.

I am truly indebted to Larry Selander and his staff for deciphering my handwritten manuscript and putting it into the modern world of computers.

I am grateful to Leon Bram for his words of wisdom; to Joe Orlandino for his care in the publishing of this book; and to Diana Haskell at the Newberry Library in Chicago for aiding me with the Illinois Ballet data, which is housed in the library's Dance Department.

To Lucia Mauro, I owe so much for her invaluable professional assistance in editing this work and the precious time involved.

Above all, I thank these dear people for their friendship, which means so much to me.

Chapter I
Richard: 1918-1945

1. Early Years. Frederic Franklin.

Richard was born on February 19, 1918 at 12 Anerley Park in southeast London during the last Zeppelin air raid on the city during World War I. His parents were Dudley Hector and Carrie Marion Ellis. He remembers little if anything of his father, who died in 1922. Richard believes that his father's death was due to injuries suffered during the war. Richard's grandfather, George Ellis, was a wine merchant in Anerley. He also died when Richard was very young, although Richard does remember visiting the wine shop. His mother, whom he believes was born in Jersey City, New Jersey, was a beautiful woman—an actress who wore stylish clothes and loved hats and boots. He recalls going to see her in her dressing room at a London theatre.

She often took Richard with her to the horse races. They would board a bus at Croydon and go to Epsom or Goodwood. Richard was always fascinated by the bookies and their sign language. He also enjoyed dirt-track racing. Every Saturday afternoon, he would go to the Crystal Palace grounds nearby to watch and, on occasion, ride with Roger Frogley, a star dirt-track racer. Richard used to practice at home on a two-stroke motorbike on the large back lawn of his home, which was on the ground floor of 12 Anerley Park. The lawn was part of the back garden surrounded by apple trees. He grew plants on a small plot there.

In his youth, Richard spent many hours on the grounds of the Crystal Palace, not only bike racing but setting up firework displays on the terrace. His job was to join the tapers together by a fuse to create a whole scene, such as the Battle of Jutland. He was also fascinated by the huge reproductions of dinosaurs scattered on islands in the park.

Dancing started when Richard was about six or seven. His mother and Gerald Ray (presumably her lover), who lived with them, used to go to a bar in the Crystal Palace Hotel. In the basement, Miss Clifton Haddan ran a ballet school, where Richard was enrolled. So while his mother was upstairs at the bar, Richard was downstairs at the barre!

His first academic school was Belvedere College in Upper Norwood. He used to walk to the faraway school and back every day. Then he transferred to Beckenham County School, where there were problems because of missing classes due to his dancing commitments. So he was transferred to a private school, where he was allowed time off to dance.

When Richard was 11 his mother died, leaving him a virtual orphan. Sadly, he has no photos or mementos of his parents or any relatives to help him remember incidents in his youth. He was left in the care of his "uncle" Gerald Ray, continuing to live in the house in Anerley. For a while in his youth, Richard and a group of closeknit young boys and girls used to play together at the Recreation grounds in Upper Norwood. They called themselves "the gang."

During that time, Richard got a good taste of the theatre. Every Monday evening, Gerald Ray would take him to the Penge Empire where they saw top musical artists performing for the Moss Empire Circuit. He saw such artists as Louis Armstrong, Cab Calloway, Wilson, Keppel and Betty, and more.

To his eternal regret, Richard missed the Diaghilev Ballet. Walking down the Strand one day, he saw an advertisement for the ballet, which was appearing for its final time at the Royal Opera House. But he didn't have enough money to buy a ticket.

Richard went to the movies quite often—to the "Two Penny Rush," as it was called. He would pay his two pennies, then stay on to see a second show. His favorite cowboy star was Tom Mix. Many of the films he saw were old silents.

Richard was doing so well at ballet and ballroom dancing winning awards, that Clifton Haddan sent him to London to further his ballet instruction at the well-known Cone School of Dance, run by three sisters, Grace, Lillian and Valerie.

While at Cone's, he continued to enter competitions. At one of them, he met Wendy Toye, now Commander of the British Empire and a renowned director of musicals and plays. Richard remembers sitting in the wings with her eating Bath buns.

Cone's used to send Richard and another young dancer to Dickens & Jones, the famous shop on Regent Street where, in the restaurant as "tea dancers," they would ask young girls to dance with them. Richard does not remember how much they were paid, if anything. He was acting, too, and at the age of 13 became a member of the London Repertory Company performing at the Regents Theatre, Kings Cross. On the programs as Dick Ellis, he was cast as a page to Sherlock Holmes in *The Speckled Band*. He was also in *Street Scene* and *Young Woodley*. In 1932 he joined the Ralph Reader Boys. Ralph Reader was a choreographer of musical shows. It was then that he met fellow dancer, Frederic Franklin. They were in a few shows together and in a film called *I Adore You*, which was being filmed at the Teddington Studios outside London, near the River Thames.

Richard and Freddie became good friends, though their friendship was put to the test one day. They went down to the Teddington locks and took out a small row boat. Freddie decided to go for a swim and jumped into the river off the boat. However, he had trouble getting back in. In his efforts to help, Richard extended an oar. But instead of helping, he accidentally hit Freddie on the head. Poor Freddie went down a couple of times, but finally got back into the boat gasping for air! He forgave Richard, and they have been close friends ever since.

Another theatrical appearance was in 1932 at the Alhambra Theatre in *A Kiss in Spring*, where Richard first came into contact with some of the top ballet dancers of the time, including Alicia Markova, Harold Turner and Frederick Ashton, who had done the choreography.

Richard also performed at the Royal Albert Hall in a program called *The Pageant of Parliament*. He giggles remembering when he and Rollo Gamble had to do a series of *brisé volés* all around the stage holding hands.

A close associate of the Cone sisters was Anton Dolin, who in January 1933 invited Richard to work with him in a show called *Ballet, Vaudeville and Variety* at the Coliseum, thus giving Richard his first ballet job. Richard appeared in *The Nightingale and the Rose* and another section of the program called *The Debutante*, with Phyllis Bedells and Harold Turner as the stars. Also appearing were Adeline Genée and Wendy Toye.

In June 1933, the Camargo Society gave a performance at the Royal Opera House. The Society had been created in 1930 in London after Serge Diaghilev's death in an effort to keep an interest in ballet alive and to provide an outlet for some of the Diaghilev dancers. It became a stepping stone for the Vic-Wells Ballet and the Ballet Rambert. At this last program, two ballets were presented: *Coppélia, Acts I and II* and *Le Lac des Cygnes, Act II* with Alicia Markova and Stanley Judson as her partner. Richard and Fred Franklyn (a misspelling in the program) were huntsmen in *Lac*, wearing what they said looked like football jerseys.

2. Vic-Wells Ballet. *Casse-Noisette*. Margot Fonteyn.

Following this performance, the Cone's told Richard that the Vic-Wells Ballet was in need of a male dancer. He was to go and see a Miss de Valois. Richard was surprised to meet a lady; he thought he was going to meet a Mr. Valois. She asked him to join the company in September 1933. His first performance was in her famous ballet, *Job*.

Also that year he was cast in the first performance of *Les Rendezvous*, a charming ballet by Frederick Ashton that is still being performed. Stanislas Idzikowski and Alicia Markova were the principal dancers. A few years later, Richard danced the male lead.

In 1934, the company presented the first performance outside of Russia of *Casse-Noisette*, later to be called *The Nutcracker*. Richard was the first Nutcracker Prince. Because he was also a guest in the Party Scene, he had to make a quick costume change. Alicia Markova starred as the Sugar Plum Fairy, surely one of the greatest, and her partner was Stanley Judson. At a later date, one of the Snowflakes was a young girl who had just joined the company. Her name was Peggy Hookham. She would change her name to Margot Fontes, her mother's maiden name, and then to Margot Fonteyn.

While she was still Peggy Hookham, Richard partnered her in *Schwanda the Bagpiper* at the Royal Opera House, thereby he was one of her first partners.

In November 1934, there was a gala performance at the Sadler's Wells Theatre of the first complete *Le Lac des Cygnes* (more commonly known as *Swan Lake*) in England. This and *Casse-Noisette* were produced by Nicholas Sergeyev, whom de Valois had found in Paris living in poverty. She arranged for him to come to London and stage *Coppélia*. For many years, Sergeyev had been *regisseur* at the Maryinsky Theatre in St.

Petersburg and had made copious notes of most of the great ballets presented there. Evidently rehearsals with Sergeyev were difficult, since he spoke very little English. Richard says he sounded like Frankenstein's monster. Many hours were spent trying to decipher what he wanted.

3. Anton Dolin. New Repertoire. Beginning of WWII

The year 1935 saw the first performance of *The Rake's Progress* choreographed by de Valois. Richard created the role of the Jockey. Walter Gore was the Rake; Alicia Markova was the Betrayed Girl. *Rake* is a significant ballet based on the William Hogarth prints, with a brilliant score by Gavin Gordon and costumes and sets by Rex Whistler. The ballet had its first performances in a season at the Shaftsbury Theatre and the Sadler's Wells sponsored by Mrs. Laura Henderson, owner of the Windmill Theatre, and her manager Vivian van Damm. During this season, Anton Dolin replaced Robert Helpmann.

Richard often recounts how Dolin usually performed one of his well-known solos, such as *Espagnol, Bolero* (to Ravel's music) or *Hymn to the Sun*, invariably improvising certain sections. Before going on stage, he would ask some of the dancers for new ideas, and they would say, "Oh, Pat, do this," or "Pat, try something like this." He was always called Pat, his real name being Patrick Healy Kay. Dolin had changed his real name, as had so many others, upon joining the Diaghilev Ballet Russe. Alicia Markova was really Alice Marks, and Ninette de Valois was Edris Stannus. Richard was always grateful to Anton Dolin, not only for giving him his first dancing job but for learning so much about partnering from him.

At the Sadler's Wells Theatre, four of the male dancers used to dress in what was the pass-room, which connected the auditorium and the stage. Many times de Valois would come through without knocking or finding out what state of dress, or undress, the men were in. All the same, Richard preferred dancing at the Sadler's Wells Theatre rather than the Old Vic Theatre, which true to its name, was old, as well as small with a poor stage surface. Its one redeeming feature: the pretty auditorium. As a rule, the company shared performances equally between the two theatres until 1936, when it left the Vic and performed only at the Wells.

One day Richard went to see the eccentric Lilian Baylis in her office to ask her for a raise. Baylis was the general manager of the Old Vic and the Sadler's Wells Theatres. In her usual fashion, she said she would have to ask God and proceeded to kneel. Then, rising, she said, "Sorry, God says no!" This had happened to other artists, too.

In 1936, five new ballets were added to the repertoire, all of which Richard appeared in: *Apparitions* and *Nocturne* choreographed by Ashton, and *Barabau, Prometheus* and *The Gods go a-Begging* by de Valois.

In 1937, *Les Patineurs* and *Wedding Bouquet*, both choreographed by Ashton were premiered (both are now in the Joffrey Ballet repertoire). That same year, de

Valois created *Checkmate*, which had its first performance in Paris at the Théâtre des Champs Elysées. Michael Somes and Richard were the original Black Knights. It was the company's first visit to France; the French were not overly enthusiastic. The following year, Ashton choreographed *Horoscope* with music by Constant Lambert, the Sadler's Wells Ballet's conductor. Fonteyn and Somes were the leads. Alan Carter and Richard were the Gemini Twins, but had to appear in the first movement before a very quick change into their Gemini costumes and makeup. Hilda Gaunt, the company pianist, usually helped them. The doubling up of roles was quite common in those days, as the company was comparatively small. Even the stars would appear in lesser roles if necessary, and with no airs and graces.

This was also a time of pioneering dance on television (although how many people had television sets then?). The company was glad to be a part of it and, although they only received a small fee, it was a welcome addition to their rather meager company salaries.

All the programs were filmed at Alexandra Palace (affectionately called "Ally Pally") in London from 1933 tp 1939. These included *Casse-Noisette*, *Le Lac des Cygnes Act II*, *Job*, *Checkmate*, *Les Patineurs*, *Les Rendezvous*, *The Gods go a-Begging*, *Wedding Bouquet*, *Nocturne*, *The Rake's Progress*, *Carnaval,* and *Façade*. Richard appeared in all of these.

The company also appeared in operas performed at the Old Vic and the Sadler's Wells Theatre. This was not always their favorite work, but some amusing moments lightened the situation.

One such occasion happened when Richard and Leslie Edwards, as spear carriers in *Aida*, were standing on either side of the stage. They wore short tunics and their dance belts. A young boy got up and went and had a look at Leslie, who then heard him say, "Coo, he ain't got no nuts!"

Another Ashton creation in 1938 was *Harlequin in the Street*. Richard created the role of the Bird Catcher.

In early 1939, the Sadler's Wells Ballet presented an ambitious full-length production of *The Sleeping Princess* staged by Nicholas Sergeyev. This ballet was choreographed by the great Marius Petipa in 1890 and was originally called *The Sleeping Beauty*. But, in 1921, Diaghilev presented a new production of the ballet and called it *The Sleeping Princess*. This, too, was staged by Sergeyev. Again, the company had a difficult time trying to understand his directions. Margot Fonteyn was Princess Aurora; Robert Helpmann was Prince Florimund and Carabosse; June Brae the Lilac Fairy. Richard was one of the Fairy's Cavaliers in the Prologue and Prince Fortune, with Ursula Moreton as Cinderella, in Act III.

While the company was on tour in 1939, passing through Leeds on September 3, they heard porters shouting that war had been declared.

The company returned to London and disbanded for a short while. Regrouping again, they went off on a provincial tour. As touring an orchestra was out of the question, Constant Lambert and Hilda Gaunt played two pianos for all the performances.

Late in 1939, the company returned to the Sadler's Wells Theatre and Ashton's new well-received ballet, *Dante Sonata*, was presented in early 1940, with the dancers in their barefeet. It was a powerful work to Liszt music.

At that time, there was a draft (call up), and unless you volunteered, you were automatically enlisted in the army. Richard, not wanting to go into the army, immediately volunteered for the Royal Navy. Miss de Valois was not happy, as she wanted to keep all the male dancers out of the services. But some of the dancers were drafted anyhow, except for Stanley Hall, who also volunteered for the Navy.

4. Tour of Holland. Cambridge.

In May 1940 the Sadler's Wells Ballet Company, as it was now named, was sent by the British Council on a short tour of Holland, opening in The Hague with a gala performance at the Royal Theatre on May 6. Further performances were given at Hengelo and Eindhoven. On the way, the company was disturbed by the number of military movements. They went back to a hotel in The Hague, as they did each night, and then proceeded to Arnhem, where they were told of the advancing German army. They saw soldiers with guns and fixed bayonets, barbed wire and other signs of preparation for war.

Les Patineurs was on the program given in Arnhem, and Richard danced the *pas de deux* with Margot. After the performance, a small girl presented de Valois with a bouquet of flowers. The young girl was Audrey Hepburn, who would suffer great deprivation during the German occupation of Holland before later becoming the beloved actress. The company left hurriedly by bus. It was an ominous journey, as trucks and tanks full of troops kept passing them in the opposite direction. The Germans entered Arnhem two hours later. Back in The Hague, the dancers were sheltered in the hotel, but some of them went up onto the roof and watched parachutists, air battles and the distant bombing of Rotterdam until things got too close, and they quickly retired inside.

They stayed in the hotel for four days during which time plans were being made to get them back to England. Meanwhile, the dancers tried to keep in practice doing barre in the hotel lounge.

News was not good and rumors abounded that they might be interred by the Germans, who now occupied much of Holland. After frantic and persistent efforts, Miss de Valois had secured the use of two buses, into which the company crammed, taking with them little luggage. Some of them wore two sets of clothes rather than leave them behind. In fact, de Valois wore Frederick Ashton's new evening suit over her own clothes. Not only were many of their personal belongings left behind, but also the costumes, sets and music from six ballets—never to be recovered. Most of the ballets were later revived, except for *Horoscope*.

The hazardous journey took the company about nine hours to arrive in Velsen. They were put up in a country house that was being used as a refugee rest center. It was overcrowded, with nowhere to sleep and no food. After tiring and nervous hours of waiting, they were finally taken by buses to Ijmuiden. On the way, they had to lie on the floor to dodge machine-gun bullets. When they reached the coast, they boarded a small cargo steamer where the only room for them was in the hold with straw on the floor. Margot and Richard lay huddled together for the whole trip. As Richard says, it was the only time he ever slept with Margot.

Their boat was escorted back to England by the destroyer taking Queen Wilhemina of Holland to safety in England. The journey took about 15 hours, landing at Harwich, from where the company took a train to London.

Gladys Trickett, de Valois' secretary, met the dancers at the station and tried to reconnect them with their families. When she saw Richard, she said she had been unable to find anyone to meet him. Richard replied, "Too bad". There wasn't anyone who could meet him. It had been a nightmare, but they were home again with no personal injuries.

Prior to Holland, the company toured extensively throughout Britain in the 1930s. In 1936, the company went to Cambridge for the first time and again in 1937 and 1938. It was always one of Richard's favorite places, especially as he found "digs" right next door to the theatre's stage door. It was during these times in Cambridge that dancers Margot Fonteyn, Pamela May and June Brae met their future husbands.

There was a time, according to Richard, when they were on tour that he and Margot dreamed of each other. They were living in different digs, and the next day would tell each other of the experience. It happened a couple of times evidently and, ever since, Margot called Richard "Dream-Boy". She wrote letters and signed photos as such. Much later, when Richard and I were married, she wrote to "Mr. & Mrs. Dream-Boy."

5. Royal Navy. Alec Guiness. Scotland.

Richard finally joined the Royal Navy in late May 1940. He went for initial training as an Ordinary Seaman to *HMS Raleigh* in Plymouth. While training, he had to be hospitailzed for a hernia. In those days, after a hernia operation, they used to make the patient sit up all night with a sheet tied under his knees and then attached to the bed posts. It was during Richard's hospital stay that there was a bad air raid on Plymouth, and one bomb dropped very close to the hospital. All the beds went flying across the room, with Richard still sitting up with the sheet tied under his knees. After that, they were all wheeled back to their places.

When he got out of the hospital, Richard was put on light duty and taught himself to type using two index fingers, which he continued to do for years. Part of his training was learning Morse Code and semaphore—the latter he said he had little trouble with as it felt like balletic *port de bras.*

While Richard was at *HMS Raleigh,* the Sadler's Wells Ballet left London because of the blitz and came to work at Dartington Hall in Devon, where choreographer Kurt Jooss had also worked. Jooss had organized his dance company in Germany in 1930. His masterpiece, *The Green Table,* won first prize at a choreographic competition in Paris. Before the war, his company came to England and made its headquarters at Dartington Hall.

Richard was able to visit the the Sadler's Wells Ballet there on a few occasions. On one such, Richard remembers an outrageous game of strip poker instigated by Bobby Helpmann.

There was another time, when Richard and one of his girlfriends were sitting on a hill near Dartmouth, when a German fighter plane flew so close to them they could clearly see the pilot and the Swastika markings on the plane. This was alarming, but the pilot simply raised his thumb and flew on.

From Plymouth, Richard was sent to Chatham, where he volunteered for submarines but was rejected because of his hernia. He was then sent to *HMS Medway Queen,* which since 1924 had been a paddle steamer sailing up and down from Tilbury in Essex to Margate in Kent. But now she was being used as a mine sweeper going ahead of slow convoys in the North Sea from the Thames to Tyne. Richard had to sit on one paddle box behind a Lewis gun. Four hours on and four hours off going chug-chug-chug.

They swept the mines by trailing two huge cables behind the paddle steamer, which cut the mine cables. When the mines came to the surface, they used rifle guns to detonate them.

During this time, his commanding officer told Richard that he had officer-like qualities and sent him to be interviewed by the captain of a large battle wagon, which Richard did. As he approached the top of the gang plank, he was met by fellow Sadler's Wells dancer Stanley Hall. Richard also had another pleasant and unexpected meeting, this time with Frederick Ashton in Newcastle in a pub. Fred was stationed there with the Royal Air Force. They planned to meet whenever the *Medway Queen* docked in Newcastle.

For his officer's training course, Richard was sent to *HMS King Alfred* at Hove near Brighton. It was there that he met Alec Guiness, whom Richard knew from the Old Vic Theatre. When Richard first saw Alec, he said "Hello Alec Guiness." Alec immediately said "Please call me Alec Cuff!," obviously wishing to be anonymous. Many years later, in 1973, Richard and I went to see Alec Guiness in London in the play *Habeus Corpus.* Richard sent him a note to his dressing room and after the show we went around to see him. At first he wasn't sure who Richard was, but then he remembered and was very friendly. They became good friends during their three months of training, not only because they were from the same organization but both were a little nervous about being commissioned. Neither of them were used to much schooling, especially in a subject like trigonometry (which seemed no problem for the young lads from Oxford and Cambridge, who made up the major part of the training course).

Alec and Richard were commissioned as Sub-Lieutenants on April 30, 1942: Alec assigned to major landing craft. Richard to a flotilla of LCA's (landing craft assault). By the time he was released from the Royal Navy in December 1945, he was a Lieutenant.

Having completed his officer's training course, Richard was sent to Inverary in Scotland, where he was in charge of training American troops for landing on beaches with eighteen landing craft known as the 550 flotilla. Each LCA held 24 men seated in three rows, with a stoker in the engine room at the stern.

While in Scotland, Richard used to jog around the camp each day to keep in shape. No one knew he was a ballet dancer. When asked, he would say he was an actor.

One time the Sadler's Wells Ballet made a tour stop in Glasgow. So Richard rode his motorbike 80 miles to Glasgow to see the company. When he got there, he was asked if he would like to perform in *Coppélia*. He went on and danced in the *Mazurka* and *Czardas,* after which he returned the 80 miles back to camp.

Another time the International Ballet came to Glasgow, and Richard rode in to see his old friend Harold Turner and Harold's future wife, Gerd Larsen. They met in a restaurant, and as it happened, I was there having tea with my company friend, Domini Callahan. We saw Richard but hardly recognized him because he had grown a beard. So strange to think that my future husband and I were in the same restaurant.

Talking about Richard's beard, he evidently decided to grow a beard while stationed in Scotland. To do this in the Navy, you had to ask permission from your commanding officer. But since Richard was the commanding officer, all he had to do was give himself permission. He had to shave it off before D-Day because he couldn't get it into a gas mask.

One day in Inverary, a young R.N. officer came up to Richard and said, "I believe you know my mother, Phyllis Bedells." Richard said, "Of course I do. I walked on with her in *The Debutante*," which reminded Richard of a time shortly after that 1932 production, when he went in for a dance competition. The two judges were Adeline Genée and Phyllis Bedells. As Richard entered the room, he said "Hello Phyllis." Evidently Genée was annoyed, thinking he should have been more respectful—not realizing that they were acquainted. Genée failed Richard by one mark.

I have written about Richard riding his motorbike from Inverary to perform in *Coppélia* with the Sadler's Wells Ballet. But there was another time in London, while he was still in the Navy and the company was performing at the New Theatre. Before a performance of *Façade*, Constant Lambert stood up at the piano and announced that Gunner Chappell (William) and Ordinary Seaman Ellis would dance the "Popular Song."

6. D-Day.

To prepare for D-Day, Richard, as commanding officer, sailed with his flotilla of 18 LCAs to Glasgow, where the boats were loaded onto train flatbeds and then taken to Plymouth. There the boats were lifted by davits onto the *Empire Anvil*, a former cargo ship docked at Plymouth.

On June 6, 1944, D-Day, they sailed in the *Empire Anvil* from Plymouth toward the French Coast, with American troops on board. Nearing the coast, the boats were lowered into the sea to set off on their mission to land the troops on the beaches.

As most people know, the weather was very stormy, and the seas were high and rough—added to which Richard had a faulty compass and went off course slightly, as others did, too, in the awful conditions. Soon realizing that something was wrong, as he didn't recognize the landscape they had studied extensively before D-Day, Richard turned his boat around. He and his flotilla sailed as fast as they could back to Omaha Beach, where the troops were to land at Fox Green. They arrived there just in time for the first wave. But many of the soldiers were seasick, and water washed over the boats. One of Richard's boats went down, and the men swam around until they were picked up by life boats and returned to the *Empire Anvil*. Many other boats sank in the rough seas, and not all the men were rescued or survived. As soon as the boats reached the beach, the troops got off through a door on the LCA that dropped open into the water and onto the beach. Going back to the *Empire Anvil* for more troops, this process continued all day, while the battlewagons were shelling at the Germans over their heads—a deafening noise. Richard remembers thinking, "What the f___ am I doing here"?! But there was no time to think about anything except getting on with the job.

Years later when Richard saw the film, *The Longest Day*, he commented that it was a "load of junk; it looked as if they were landing in Lake Michigan." I wonder if any other ballet dancer was in command of a flotilla of landing craft that transported American troops onto Omaha Beach on D-Day? Richard didn't exactly feel like doing a double *tour en l'air*!

7. Duty in Holland. End of War.

After the D-Day invasion, Richard's flotilla was lessened to 12 landing craft and taken to Holland, where they were loaded onto trucks and taken to a canal near Flushing.

They were stationed in a nice little town named Goes (Hoos). Here their main job was transporting, by landing craft, Lord Lovat and as Richard called them, his crazy Scouts, up and down the Scheldt for various raids against the Germans. Early on, Richard had to go on a reconnaissance flight of the sand bars in the Scheldt. He flew in a two-stroke mono two-seater plane with just the pilot and himself. The pilot told Richard quite blithely that the plane might roll over on landing. Fortunately it didn't, but it was quite a nerve-wracking experience anyhow.

The flotilla would do eight-hour shifts and, during some of this time, the weather was very cold. To keep warm, Richard said he wore a Balaklava helmet with a tin hat on top and a duffel coat with a hood looking like the Michelin Tire man.

One day they did an assault on Flushing. Allegedly, there was a German sniper firing at them from a windmill. A bullet whizzed right under Richard's nose. He said it sounded like an angry wasp. Another bullet ricocheted off a silver flask that he kept in his back pocket. Luckily it only dented the flask, not Richard's derriere! He still has the flask, dent and all.

Another time, Richard and his flotilla captured a miniature German submarine and crew which had run aground. The captain, on being captured, spat in Richard's face. One of Richard's officers had to restrain him from hitting the man in retaliation, as hitting a prisoner was a punishable offense.

The men in the flotilla had a jeep for traveling around in, but they also bought an old car from the Burgomaster of a town, called Bergen-op-Zoom, for a bottle of Scotch. One day Richard's second in command was driving the car with Richard sitting in the back. The officer suddenly turned to Richard and said, "Do you want to take the wheel?" Richard said, "Yes, alright." With that, the man took the wheel off and handed it to Richard!

There was a time in Goes when the flotilla was told of a possible German breakthrough and that they were right in line for such an attack, but fortunately the Germans were halted.

Richard and a few other officers were sent to Middleburg, and on their return to Goes, and they found the flotilla had been recalled to England and his second in command had taken most of the flotilla back.

So after many months in Holland, Richard and the remaining officers and men returned to England, where they waited around expecting any day to be sent to help in the Pacific war. But, thankfully, that never happened as the war ended in August.

Richard served in the Royal Navy from May 1940 until December 1945 and was released on February 13, 1946. During this time he had received the 1939-1945 Star, the France-Germany Star, the 1939-1945 Medal, the Atlantic bar, the Defense Medal and a Mentioned in Dispatches. On leaving the Navy, all he got was a suit.

8. Richard in London.

For a time before the war, while he was at Sadler's Wells, Richard lived alone at 10 Roland Gardens in London in a tiny flat on the top floor, where he was able to lie in bed and look at the stars through a skylight. He had a very small bathroom and a gas ring to cook on. It was while he was at Roland Gardens that Richard first met Denis Rake, who owned the house opposite. Denis, who was older than Richard, had led a fascinating life and was to lead an even more fascinating one during the war when he worked in France for the Special Operations Executive. Born in Brussels, he was a child circus performer and a musical comedy star before joining the SOE later in life.

Speaking French fluently, he was sent to France as a radio operator to help the Marquis (underground army) obtain arms from England. Denis' job was to radio to London for supplies and instructions, which he did under dangerous conditions. He wrote a book, *Rake's Progress*, about his life before joining the SOE and during that remarkable time. During the war, if Richard found that Denis was in London, they would meet at Pastori Hotel in Leicester Square. It was a hot bed of secret agents and somehow managed to obtain large amounts of meat, despite the harsh rationing. Richard remembers times when they would hear that an inspector was arriving, and huge sides of beef were seen being hurriedly carried to a hiding place

During some of these war time leaves in London, Richard said if the air raid sirens went off as he walked down the street and bombs started to drop, he would lie down in the nearest gutter, clean or otherwise, as most people did. Then he would find the nearest pub, refusing to go to an underground shelter, preferring to have a glass in his hand if his time was up.

On one of his leaves, Denis was in a pub with Richard and started to talk about his latest job. In war time, it was forbidden to discuss your war work with anyone unless it was a close relative. Evidently someone, on this occasion, reported Denis to the authorities. On arriving back at his base, Denis was placed under close arrest. At the same time, Richard was too, not knowing what was going on. The only way that Denis could get out of the situation was to claim Richard as his adopted son—which, age-wise, was possible. But from then on, that fact stayed on Denis' official papers. Much later, after the war, Denis went to work for Douglas Fairbanks, Jr., and for screening purposes, to obtain the job, Douglas saw Denis' papers, his army records and noticed that he had a "son." Incidentally, Douglas wrote the Foreword for Denis' book.

Years later, when he was performing in Chicago in *The Pleasure of His Company*, we went to see Douglas, and he asked after Richard's "father." He asked his dresser to take a photo of the three of us, saying he would send a copy to Denis.

Chapter II
Christine: 1923-1945

1. Family. Early Years. Palestine.

I was born on June 12, 1923 in a private nursing home run by an Irish friend of my mother's at Grange Park in Ealing, London. My father, Guy George Houssemayne-Du Boulay, was English of Huguenot descent and a Royal Air Force pilot. He met my mother, Raby Violet Emmeline Knox, in Ireland during the Black and Tan Revolts. My parents were not able to get married until my mother came of age because her father, Godfrey Knox, objected to the union. So on reaching the age of 21 in July 1922, my mother came to England, and she and my father were married on August 3 at St. Mary's Church in East Grinstead, Sussex. East Grinstead was where my paternal grandparents lived. My grandfather, Ralph Houssemayne-Du Boulay (one of 13 children), was educated at Winchester College, where his father had been a housemaster and who later had a house at Winchester College named after him. For a time my grandfather was in the Egyptian Government Service. Before her marriage, my grandmother was Ethel Margaret Thurston. They had four children: my father, Alison Mary, Joan Thurston and Louise Marguerite. The male branch of my side of the family came to an end as I was my parents' only child. Alison never married. Joan married Robert Burton, and they had one child, Jillian, who came to America and met her husband, Mitch Hrushowy. They had one child, Michelle. Peggy married Geoffrey Bond, and they also had one child, Jane.

On my maternal side, my grandfather had two daughters by his first wife who died. He then married Mary Butler White, and their only child was my mother. My maternal grandmother was a direct descendant of the Handcock family. Her grandmother had been a Butler. One of her cousins was poet William Butler Yeats. She was a very accomplished water colorist, and happily I have some of her paintings.

In 1796, the Handcocks purchased a lovely 45-acre estate called Sally Park at the foot of the Wicklow Hills, near the town of Templeogue outside Dublin. It consisted of a large house approached through big wrought-iron gates with a gate lodge, then up a long driveway. In front of the house stretched an expansive lawn beyond which was a large, beautiful garden. At one side of the house, there was a long greenhouse, where my grandfather grew magnificent begonias. These and the gladioli he grew won many top prizes at the Dublin Flower Show. The property was also comprised of three large fields, two ponds (one of which had swans on it), several barns and a dairy.

Sally Park had been left to my grandmother, who bequeathed it to my grandfather on her death, which was before my mother was married. My grandfather was of the Knox family from County Mayo, whose family tree dates back to the 15th century. His first cousin was Major Lawrence E. Knox, the founder of the *Irish Times* in 1859.

From the time I was one year old, I went to Sally Park with my mother at least once a year. It was fairly isolated, most of the other large homes being quite a distance away, and transport was not easy. Therefore, I did not see many children my age, except the children of our wonderful servants who lived in the village of Firhouse, where Sally Park was situated. We had a cook, housemaid, gardener, yardman and a couple who lived in the gate lodge. So I played with their children most of the time and they became my friends. There were about five, and they were all wonderful Irish dancers. They would often dance for my mother and me on the large kitchen floor. I loved watching them.

One of my favorite places in Sally Park was called the Primrose Path, a long path with a large field on one side and a line of trees on the other. In the spring, the banks on both sides were smothered in primroses and bluebells. Looking beyong the field, one could see the Wicklow Mountains and their ever-changing hues of blue. Another special place was the formal rose garden consisting of many beds, each edged with low-level box hedges and a sun dial in the center of them all. I remember with delight, when the roses were in bloom, my mother and I would cut bunches of them each day.

Those early days when I stayed there were quite primitive. I remember we had gas light and oil lamps, and the villagers had outhouses. When we finally got electricity, we had our first telephone, and the radio was housed in a huge piece of furniture.

I remember my grandfather getting a car, one of the early Austins I believe. My grandfather died in the mid-1930s and left Sally Park to his three daughters. So its contents were divided into three. But since two were married and living in South Africa, it was left to my mother to manage everything. Much as she loved Sally Park, she had no wish to keep it. Eventually it was sold.

My early years in England were spent moving about, with my father in the Royal Air Force and stationed at different aerodromes. He was born on Friday, October 13, 1899 in Egypt when my grandfather was working there. After the birth of my aunts Alison and Joan, the family returned to England.

In 1912, my father entered Lancing College on a classical scholarship and remained there for five years. Then, faking his age, he joined the Royal Flying Corps, then the RAF, and was stationed in the Middle East. In 1919, he was invalided out and sent to Ireland from 1920 to 1921. It was there that he met my mother.

He rejoined the RAF and was commissioned in 1923. From 1925 to 1927, he was back in Palestine and Iraq. During this period, my mother and I sailed out to Palestine to see him. I remember passing through the Bay of Biscay, notorious for storms, where we hit a bad one and most of the passengers were sick—but not me. I stayed on deck with the crew.

For six months, we lived in a bungalow near Jaffa. Our servant Hussein used to take me for donkey rides and once on a camel. He taught me some Arabic, so I used to try to speak to the locals. I saw lepers in the streets of Jaffa and oranges growing on the trees. We had a tortoise named Jeremiah and a dachshund named Bertie, who was actually the squadron's mascot. My father loved that dog. All these are things that have stuck in my mind.

My parents had not been getting on well together and, on our return to England, they separated.

I stayed with my mother, and we returned to Ealing, a western suburb of London. Ealing Broadway is well known and is the end of the line for some Underground trains.

For a few years in her youth, Margot Fonteyn lived in Ealing and went to ballet classes there.

My mother and I lived in a small flat, as we didn't have too much money. I went to kindergarten at a private school called Harvington, where I stayed until I was 15 years old. After a year or so, we moved to a nice flat in a big old house at 4 Glastonbury Mansions on Grange Road, off which was Grange Park where I was born. It was on the corner of the main road to Kew Gardens. Across that road was Ealing Green and nearby was Walpole Park, where Ealing Film Studios used to be.

The house had a large garden which made my mother happy, she missed the one at Sally Park. My mother and I spent the better part of a year at Sally Park after my parents' separation. In fact we spent all our summer holidays there, until I left Harvington.

In the mid-1930s, my mother and I were invited out a couple of times by Marion Holden. Marion, I have since learned, was a close friend of my father's. She was married and lived with her husband, a millionaire, which was real wealth in those days. Why Marion befriended my mother I am not sure, but she always very kind. One time she took us to lunch at the famous Embassy Club in London, where we sat in a booth next to the one where C.B. Cochran was lunching. Cochran produced extravagant revues. I remember, too, how my eyes nearly popped out of my head when the dessert tray was wheeled our way. I had never seen so many delicacies. Marion then took us to a famous bookstore and bought me two beautiful books.

In the two-floor flat above ours lived Hilary Greenfield and her elderly grandmother, who died soon after we met. We became close friends with Hilary; she was an artist, an excellent gardener and an avid ballet fan. So we had much in common. Soon after her grandmother died, she suggested we move upstairs and live with her. There was plenty of room, and she had use of the major part of the garden.

So we moved upstairs. It worked out very well and we were happy.

2. Ballet Companies.

Hilary's love of ballet was contagious. On many occasions, she and my mother took me to see ballet performances. We attended the Sadler's Wells Ballet, Markova-Dolin company, Massine's Ballet Russe de Monte Carlo, the Jooss ballet, Colonel de Basil's company, the Ballet Club and many more. How fortunate I was. I learned so much about style and presentation from watching great stars of the ballet world during the mid- to late 1930s. We saw de Basil's famous "baby ballerinas": Tamara Toumanova, Tatiana Riabouchinska and Irina Baronova; also the legendary Alexandra Danilova, the great dancer and choreographer Léonide Massine, Leon Woizikowski, Paul Petrov,

Nina Nemchinova and others. The de Basil company performances typically took place at the Royal Opera House in Covent Garden. Since we could not afford good seats, we got tickets for the "gods", as the top balcony was called. To get your ticket, you had to go to the theatre early the morning of the performance and queue. The wait was often long, but folding stools helped. During the wait, buskers, or street artists, would come by on Floral Street and perform for us. Some were quite entertaining.

Then in the evening, armed with your ticket—it was first come, first served—once the doors were opened, you joined the mad dash up the many flights of stairs and scrambled for a good seat. This was depicted very well in the film *The Red Shoes*. There is another scene in the film, of the Ballet Club performing in the little Mercury Theatre in Notting Hill. My mother, Hil and I went there many times. It was remarkable how Marie Rambert, the director, was able to present so many exciting programs on the tiny stage. But she and the dancers managed, performing some of the early works of Anthony Tudor and Frederick Ashton, whose ballets would become classics. The first ballet performance I ever saw was by the Vic-Wells Ballet at the Sadler's Wells Theatre. *The Jackdaw and the Pigeons*, *Fête Polonaise* and *The Jar* made up that program.

The Markova-Dolin company performed at the King's Theatre, Hammersmith, quite often. Hammersmith being fairly close to Ealing, we saw the company as much as we could and I became a big fan of Frederic Franklin. He was such a delightful and exuberant dancer. I used to beg my mother and Hilary to let me stand at the stage door to see the dancers and sometimes get their autographs in my book. I got two signed photos from Fred.

I continued with my academic studies at Harvington, where I did well in art classes. I received high marks and encouragement from a dear lady, who came once a week to give two or three of us special painting classes, including *en plein* (all in watercolors) when the weather was good enough to be outside. I also got top marks in some national art competitions. I received encouragement, too, from Hil, who was an artist. She also worked mainly in watercolors. One of them, a painting of Markova as the Betrayed Girl in *The Rake's Progress*, was on the cover of an issue of *The Dancing Times*. Another we have hanging in our home is of Nijinsky in *Le Spectre de la Rose*.

3. Beginning Ballet. Sadler's Wells Ballet School. Ballet Teachers.

A former student at Harvington, Joan Durrant, gave dancing classes there, which I attended. She was also teaching at Doris Stainer's school of ballet in South Kensington. Joan told my mother that she would like me to attend a weekly class at Miss Stainer's for more serious study, which I did. I enjoyed my ballet classes and loved my uniform, a small white costume with a fairly full short skirt. Miss Stainer, by the way, was Leslie Howard's sister. Leslie is perhaps best known for his role in the film, *Gone with the Wind*.

Part of my training at Miss Stainer's was to prepare for and take Cecchetti Society Ballet Examinations. I took my first one in 1938. I failed. It was awful. I had a list of 13 faults on my exam result paper. I should have given up there and then. But I think it made me more determined than ever to do well. There was a girl in the class above mine who went to an audition for the Vic-Wells Ballet School and was accepted. I thought if she can, so can I!

My mother arranged for an audition for me at the Sadler's Wells Theatre, where I was auditioned with two other girls by Ursula Moreton. This was in early summer, just after I had left school. Oh joy! Miss Moreton told my mother I could join the school when it reopened in September. Meanwhile, she suggested I go for ballet classes with Anna Pruzina. This I did and learned a lot and enjoyed working with and meeting some professional dancers. So I didn't start serious ballet training until I was just 15, which is considered late by most standards.

During this time, I was also taking weekly private lessons in French. How I wish I had kept this up and remembered more. It was an enjoyable summer free of school, which I hated once I got involved in ballet. I was so happy the day I finished that I took my school uniform and dumped it into the garbage bin at the end of the garden. In September, I became a student at the Sadler's Wells School of Ballet, which was ideally located in the theatre. Our classes were held in the Board Room and in the Wells Room, where the company worked most of the time. Richard often remarks on how amazing it was that anything could be rehearsed in the Wells Room. During performances, it was used for refreshments. During the day, it served as the company class and rehearsal room. It wasn't very large and was obstructed by columns, making it difficult to maneuver in the corps-de-ballet moves for ballets, such as *The Sleeping Princess* and *Le Lac des Cygnes*.

We students would sometimes creep into the theatre auditorium and watch stage rehearsals or see company members as we moved about the theatre building. How lucky we were.

I never had the ideally arched ballet feet. In fact, I was pigeon-toed as a young child. Dancing helped to correct this, and soon after joining the Wells School, I was told I could try a little pointe work. But I still wasn't ready. They took me off pointe and sent me to an orthopedic specialist, who helped me so much that, a year later, I was on pointe again with no trouble. Fortunately, I never had any trouble with my feet throughout my performing years, and for the last years wore no padding for my toes.

While I was a student at the Wells, I received two progress reports, one in early 1939 and one in June of that year, both written by Miss de Valois. Both were encouraging with constructive criticisms. I always felt that she liked me not so much for my dancing, but that I was half Irish and the other half was Huguenot, as was she.

One of my teachers was Nicholas Sergeyev, and I did not like his classes. He was a bit of a tyrant and taught using a stick. While we were doing *developpés* for 16 counts in each position *en croix*, he would invariably come along and keep tapping my thigh with his stick saying, "Allez, Allez, keep keep." I bruised very easily and was not happy.

Other teachers I had in the school were Ailne Phillips, Sheila McCarthy, Joy Newton and de Valois herself. I was always scared in her classes, mostly because of who she was.

Also, her classes usually concentrated on fast, tricky little steps, or *petit allegro*, which I was not good at then. So I struggled, knowing it was essential to my training. It was under de Valois' guidance that the Sadler's Wells became known for the company's excellent footwork. Another teacher was Ursula Moreton, whom I loved, especially as she taught wonderful character classes, which I really enjoyed and did well in. Ursula, having been in the Diaghilev Ballet, had learned from some of the great Russian character dancers. She was truly knowledgeable on the subject and able to hand down this great tradition to us students. It's interesting to note that none of these teachers wore special dance outfits to teach in. They all wore their everyday clothes. They didn't "perform" to show us what to do.

4. Art Classes. *The Sleeping Princess.*

To get to the theatre from my home in Ealing, I took the Underground train to Holborn and then transferred to the bus, which stopped at the theatre. The Central School of Arts and Crafts was located at Holborn. So I signed up for classes there in architecture and costume design, with thoughts of being a stage designer if not a dancer.

I had always been aware of Richard Ellis, having seen him in many performances and quite a few times with other company members around the theatre. Then one day, as I was going home down the long escalator at the Holborn Station, Richard passed me. As he was on the up escalator, he turned, saw me and smiled. I couldn't believe he had noticed a student.

After the first few performances of the new production of *The Sleeping Princess* in 1939, I was thrilled to be one of the pages to the King and Queen in the first and third acts. On March 22, 1939, the Vic-Wells Ballet gave a gala performance at the Royal Opera House to honor the French President and his wife. The first and third acts of *The Sleeping Princess* were presented, with Sir Thomas Beecham conducting, and I was on as a page. How exciting to be in the great Opera House. It also was the first time that Richard's and my name appeared on a program for a performance at the Opera House. Incidentally March 22 would be a significant date in our lives.

At that time, the news about Germany was troubling. We were being prepared for war, with all civilians being issued gas masks.

5. Ireland. Outbreak of WWII.

In late June of 1939, the ballet school was closed for the summer months. My mother and I left for our annual trip to Ireland. But with Sally Park being sold after my grandfather's death, we stayed with Lizzy, a family servant in her small house near Sally Park. In July, we went on our annual visit to Cortoon in northwest County Mayo.

Cortoon was the name of the property where my great aunt Adelaide (Addie) Gardiner, lived. She was a dear elderly lady. A heavenly and secluded place, Cortoon was situated on a tiny peninsula near the ocean. The house had a thatched roof, mullioned windows and, over the thatched canopy, clematis and fuschia intermingled. Across the path to the front door, a few steps led down to a pebbly, seaweedy beach. At high tide, the water came right up to the top step. The only way to reach Cortoon was by boat or a long rutted road that led to the main road to Killala. We traveled this way by pony and trap, passing nearby woods carpeted with daffodils in the spring. It was here, while returning from rowing a boat around in front of the house, that I heard the news that war had been declared. It seemed so impossible in such an isolated and lovely place.

My mother and I returned to Dublin and continued to stay near Sally Park with Lizzy. Meanwhile, my mother wrote to Ninette de Valois and asked for her advice. She wrote back saying that, for the time being, the school was closed. But a trusted ex-dancer, Sara Payne—who, as Sara Patrick, had worked with de Valois at the Abbey Theatre—was now living and teaching in Dublin. She suggested I take classes with her until things settled down.

I joined Sara's small school and performing group. Jill Gregory, a member of the Sadler's Wells Ballet, was also there working with Sara. We studied daily and performed quite often in individual productions and operas. Especially delightful were the programs we did at the Gate Theatre operated by Lord and Lady Longford. There were many reasons for this. The wardrobe mistress for the Gate acting company was Nancy Beck, a former classmate of my mother's. It was a nice reunion. Nancy introduced me to Carl Bonn, the company stage and costume designer. Hearing of my interests, he offered to give me classes. Carl was an excellent teacher, and I loved my lessons with him. He would choose plays of different periods, for instance Shakespeare's *Love's Labour Lost*, Turguenev's *A Month in the Country* or Sheridan's *School for Scandal*, and asked me to design costumes and sets for these plays. Then he would critique them, teaching me so much about the history of costuming. I still have all those designs.

I also found my first love at the Gate: one of the lead actors. I was in the theatre a lot in those days.

6. Return to London. New Theatre.

Nevertheless, with news of the war and the London blitz, worries over Hilary staying alone in Ealing, and a touch of homesickness, my mother and I decided to return home. So early in 1942 we returned to London.

I immediately hurried back to the Sadler's Wells School, where classes and rehearsals were now held in two newly built studios with mirrors—though we were not allowed to use them too much, only on occasions to help with correcting positions or to ensure exact moves of two or more dancers. I was promoted after two days to the advanced class. At the school, we were encouraged to take Royal Academy of Dancing exams. I had taken one when I was in Ireland and had received honors. This time, I just failed getting honors. But I was not too dismayed after I was told that Margot Fonteyn had failed her exam. In retrospect, I am very glad I took the R.A.D. exams because their extensive list of steps and theory of movements in ballet were indispensable to me when I later became a teacher.

The Sadler's Wells Ballet Company was performing at the New Theatre in London then because the Sadler's Wells Theatre had been taken over as a shelter for air-raid victims. The Old Vic Theatre Company also was appearing there. Happily, I was chosen as an apprentice and appeared in performances of *The Sleeping Princess* and *Giselle* and was also able to see some of the Old Vic theatre productions, memorably Laurence Olivier in his magnificent double bill of *Oedipus Rex* and *The Critic*.

I was asked to join the company for a proposed tour of South America, but it never materialized. Then I received my call-up (draft) papers. Naturally, I was concerned about my career. I thought, if worse came to the worse, my father might be able to pull a few strings and get me into an interesting war job. But as luck would have it, an ex-classmate of mine from the ballet school, who was in the International Ballet, told me they were holding auditions. I went and was accepted.

7. International Ballet. Touring. Hitler's V-1's and V-2's. V-E Day.

The International Ballet was a fairly new company run by Mr. and Mrs. Inglesby mainly as a vehicle for their daughter, Mona, the company's star. Somehow they were able to keep most of their dancers out of the services.

The company was well run and well presented, with no skimping or shabbiness about it. And Mrs. Inglesby saw to that. If she ever saw you sitting on your costumes, there was hell to pay. In later years, when I was making the costumes for our company, I could fully appreciate why.

I joined the company in Blackpool and vividly remember my first appearance as a Wili in the second act of *Giselle*. I learned the steps from one other girl in the corridor of the dressing rooms. (On Richard's first tour, they went to Blackpool.) The repertoire was mostly classical, with a few ballets choreographed by Mona. Most of them were good. Though, as with her dancing, they just missed greatness.

The company consisted of some very accomplished dancers. Harold Turner, having left the Sadler's Wells company, was the lead male dancer, a great asset. He also choreographed a ballet for the company, *Fête Bohème*, which I enjoyed performing in.

The studios were located in South Kensington, where we rehearsed and had daily classes. We were so fortunate to have Stanislas Idzikowski as our ballet master. "Idzi," a short and dapper man, wore a suit, waistcoat and his outdoor shoes while teaching. His pianist-companion, Madam Evina, accompanied all his classes. Of course, having been a pupil of Enrico Cecchetti, the famous teacher of Anna Pavlova and others, Idzi maintained a strict Cecchetti class regimen, adhering to much the same class every week day. This repetition, if sometimes tedious, was ultimately a good thing, as it helped in perfecting movements.

Going to class one day after a V-1 attack, I emerged from South Kensington Station to find chaos. A bomb had landed near the station. I had to walk over rubble and debris to get to the studio nearby, which was not damaged. The V-1, or "doodle bug" as we called it, was the flying bomb that Hitler launched against London. This was followed by another deadly missile, the V-2, which landed without any warning at all.

The International Ballet toured quite extensively all over England, Scotland and Wales in many different theatres. The old ones invariably had "raked" stages, which were hard for dancers because they had to quickly adjust their equilibrium, especially when performing pirouettes. One old theatre was not a favorite. We had to trudge up three flights of steps to the *corps-de-ballet* dressing-room. So up and down we went. Rather exhausting, all the more so if we had to make a quick change of costumes during a ballet. Only the "stars" were allowed to change at stage level.

One place I did love visiting was Edinburgh—so beautiful and historic, in particular Princes Street and the dramatic Edinburgh Castle atop its high hill. All the same, it was there that I sustained the only injury I ever experienced during my dancing days. After visiting the Castle, I tripped and fell, turning my ankle. The swelling and pain resulted in my missing a performance.

As with most touring companies, we kept a list of digs. We used to write ahead of time to make our reservations. Sometimes we had to write to unknown addresses and often would receive an answer written with abbreviated information—"vacant/double front and one single back—no meals," referring to a double bed in the front of the house and a single bed at the back and no meals. Some of the land ladies, though, were wonderful cooks despite the harsh rationing. Some had guest books, which we would scan to see if any of our friends or a well-known person had stayed in the same digs. When we weren't able to make prior bookings, we would leave the station and trek through the streets, suitcases in hand, trying to find a place to stay. In bad weather, we were usually forced to take the first vacancy. In the cold weather most digs had little, if any, heat. Occasionally, there would be a coal fire in the rooms or a gas fire with a meter, which had to be fed with a shilling or two. None of these warmed the whole room, especially when most of the floors were bare linoleum. The bathrooms were primitive, too, the hot water coming from a small gas geyser or, worse, a landlady would bring a jug of hot water to your room so you could wash in the small basin provided. There was no such thing as a shower. We always said one of the reasons we came to America was to be able to have a shower in our house.

I mentioned rationing, which many people remember as quite severe during the war. We had very little butter, sugar, bread or milk; and the meat ration amounted to one small steak per week. So we resorted to no milk or sugar in our tea for one thing and ate chicken and rabbit for our meat supply, augmented on occasion with horsemeat and lots of sausages, which we swore were mostly filled with seasoned sawdust. We hardly ever saw oranges or bananas.

Clothing was rationed too. So we coined the phrase "make-do-and-mend". My mother, an expert seamstress, did this very well and made most of my clothes. After the war, many of us pulled down our black-out curtains to make longer skirts for ourselves. The necessity of saving material and wearing short skirts was over, and long was the fashion. Years later, seeing the hilarious skit with Carol Burnett as Scarlett O'Hara making a dress from the drapes, reminded me of our desperate efforts.

When I first joined the International Ballet, I shared digs with Domini Callahan. She had been a fellow student with me in 1939. Another student at that time had been Barbara Fallis, who would later marry Richard Thomas and become the mother of Richard Thomas, the well-known actor.

After Domini left the company, I used to dig with dancer Moira Tucker.

If we were passing through London while on a tour, I would go home for the night—often bringing a friend or two with me. Sonia Arova often stayed with me. We had fun in the dormitory my mother set up for us. Sonia later reached ballerina status and danced with many major companies.

When we were appearing in London, again I would stay at home in Ealing, taking the Tube to one of the Ealing stations, either Ealing Broadway or South Ealing.

One night, after the performance, I realized there was a bad fog. I got the train hoping it would not be too bad when I arrived at South Ealing. When I got off the train it was worse—a real "pea-souper." Normally, if the weather was bad, I caught a bus rather than walk the short distance home. But this night, nothing was running—no buses, no cars—of course no lights because of the black-out. There was nothing to do but try to find my way home. As I left the station, someone in front of me carried a torch (flashlight). So I followed closely, which helped, until he turned down a side street. Alone in total darkness, I had to literally feel my way along until I knew I had to cross the main road. I finally reached home safely after this frightening ordeal. I understand that "pea soupers" are supposed to be a thing of the past, as the government banned the use of coal in fireplaces, believed to be one of the main causes.

Even without "pea soupers," traveling at night was difficult. All the buses and trains had thick netting on the windows to guard against bomb blasts. There was just a small diamond-shaped opening on each window, through which—if you were lucky—you could see the station name. But once the trains were out in the open and not underground, the station names were impossible to see because of the black-out, and the diamond openings never seemed to line up with the station name. Occasionally people would make a tear in the mesh in an effort to see better. There were printed slogans on the trains featuring a character called "Billy Brown of London Town." One such slogan read, "Please pardon my correction, but that stuff is there for your protection."

Richard was on the train one day when he saw that someone had written beside this sign, "Thanks so much for the information, but I can't see the f____g station"!

On a more serious note, during the war, many people decided to seek shelter in the Underground stations, either because they had been bombed out of their homes and had nowhere to sleep or feared being bombed.

Each night, after performing in a theatre in London and taking the train home to Ealing, I would walk along the platform crowded with men, women and children trying to find a place to sleep for another night away from the terror: at that time, of the V-1 or the V-2 flying bombs. One day sitting in our garden in Ealing, my mother, Hil and I, heard a "doodle-bug" approaching and were horrified to see it not just passing by, but stop and spiral down out of control. It, fortunately, missed us.

It sounded like a motorbike and suddenly the engine would stop. It was then that it would drop to the ground. If we were out walking and heard or saw one, we would lie down on the ground to avoid, if possible, the worst of any blast.

In 1944 from August 28 to October 7, the International Ballet performed at the Adelphi Theatre on the Strand in London. In the middle of the ballet, *Twelfth Night*, we heard a "doodle bug" stop overhead, meaning that it might drop right by us. But Leslie French, the actor who performed with us and was appearing in *Twelfth Night*, paused for a second and then continued with his speech as if nothing had happened—a reassuring moment for all of us, the audience included. It happened again during a performance of *Les Sylphides*. Scary moments, but what could we do but keep going. All the same, it was during this time that the Allies had already started their offensive against Hitler and his dreadful regime of destruction of people and property. We were retaliating.

I remember soon after D Day, walking along near Marble Arch and watching the sky cloud over, as hundreds of huge bombers were flying eastward, obviously on their mission to bomb German cities. It was quite a sight.

Happily all this horror ended for us on V-E Day, May 8, 1945. The ballet company was on tour in Plymouth that day. Some of us had gone to Cawsand—it was a day off and a lovely one. On our way back, we realized something special had happened. The harbour was full of boats of all sizes hooting, flying flags and bells ringing—a heartwarming scene. It seemed so long ago that we were on tour in Southsea on England's south coast in 1944. It was my 21st birthday, and I was feeling homesick. So I went for a walk down to the sea and was amazed to see all the ships and men preparing, as I was to find out later, to go to France and continue the invasion.

A couple of times, I had approached Miss de Valois about joining her company. But she wisely told me I was obligated to the Inglesbys, as they were keeping me out of the services. Yet she said when the war was over, she would certainly consider taking me.

The Inglesbys treated me well and gave me some nice things to do, including Olivia in *Twelfth Night* and Prayer in *Coppélia*. They had arranged for Sergeyev to stage the full-length *Coppélia* for the company. No classes, thank goodness! But I loved *Coppélia* and still think it was one of my favorites to perform. At that time I was one of Swanilda's friends.

I was often cast in the famous *pas de quatre* in Act II of *Le Lac des Cygnes*, which was always a challenge, especially so one day when I committed a ballet "no-no." I had not tied my shoe ribbons securely enough, and they came undone on one shoe during the series of little *jetés*. I was desperate, but had to keep going of course. I was able to kick off the shoe. Fortunately, it landed near my friend, Sonia Arova, who was standing as a *corps* girl beside the wings. She was able to surreptitiously push it into the wings while I completed the dance with one shoe. The audience evidently appreciated my predicament and applauded loudly. Miss Inglesby did not.

After V-E Day, I went to see Miss de Valois and told her that my contract with the International Ballet was up in December, 1945. She said that it was good timing as the company was moving to the Royal Opera House, opening with *The Sleeping Beauty* in February, and she needed extra dancers. Rehearsals were to begin on January 2, 1946, and she asked me to join the company then.

Richard, aged 9, with
competition medals.

Richard with William Chappell and Pearl Argyle in *The Gods Go A-Begging*.

Sally Park.

Richard in the Royal Navy in Holland.

Myself in Palestine.

The "Rose Adagio." Richard, Pauline Clayden, Harold Turner, Anthony Burke, Margot Fonteyn.

Little house in Ealing where
Richard proposed.

Myself with Frederic Franklin and Denis Rake
on Cannes beach.

Harold Turner, Margot Fonteyn, Pamela May, Frederick Ashton,
and Gerd Larsen at our wedding.

Villa at Cap Ferrat (tall building, center).

Chapter III
Sadler's Wells Ballet: 1946-1949

1. Royal Opera House. Meeting Richard. Robert Helpmann.

So after three years, I left the International Ballet and joined the Sadler's Wells Ballet—an exciting move because the beautiful Opera House would be our "home."

Rehearsals began for *The Sleeping Beauty*, as it was now called, and Richard, who was only a few weeks out of the Navy and still in uniform, rejoined the company.

He said he went to the Opera House as soon as he could after being "demobbed," and the first person he saw was de Valois. She said, "Oh Eric! (for some unknown reason, she often called him Eric) How nice to see you. Now what can you do?" Richard replied, "Madam (as she was affectionately called), I have only just left the Navy after five and a half years in the war. I don't think I can do anything much." She said, "Don't be silly boy, of course you can!" He was back in the company, expected to do *entrechat six* and *double tours* as if he had never gone off to fight a war. Naturally it was hard for him to get back into practice. He started slowly, just doing barre work, gradually building up his strength. To help the process, he used to go to classes with the legendary Vera Volkova, where many of the company dancers went, including Fonteyn. But being out of condition, the stresses and strains caught up with him and he sustained a few minor injuries. He remained a soloist, but felt he never regained the technique he had before the war.

I think Richard and I began our friendship when we found ourselves on the same train doing crosswords. I had always been addicted to crosswords—hereditary, I think, as my father used to have little trouble doing the ones in the *London Times*.

After that, Richard and I went out together quite often. But early on, I was not all that receptive to his advances. I was still missing my actor-friend in Dublin. When I realized that would never work out, Richard and I became very close. Richard was living in a flat in Bina Gardens near Gloucester Road. Denis Rake had found the flat and furnished it with his things and a few of Richard's items, which had been stored during the war, so that when Richard came out of the Navy, he had somewhere to live. Denis was not there; he was working in the passport division of the British Embassy in Paris. I remember the first time Richard took me to the flat. He cooked us dinner on a tiny gas ring. We had steak (obtained with the help of Denis' ration book), peas and potatoes—quite a feast in those days.

After we became lovers, I tried to stay at the flat as often as I could. But it wasn't easy. I hated having to lie to my mother about my whereabouts. Richard remembers Fred Ashton turning to him one day saying, "I see you have started again!" Richard had had the reputation of liking the girls.

The Sleeping Beauty was a great success. Their Royal Highnesses the King and Queen and the two young Princesses sat in the Royal Box. The beautiful auditorium was once more filled with a glamorous, elegantly dressed audience not seen since before the war.

The dancers were well dressed, too, in the gorgeous costumes and magnificent scenery designed by Oliver Messel. How this was ever achieved is almost a miracle, as there was still rationing of every sort and, in some cases, it was worse after the war ended. Messel was present at many of our fittings and rehearsals to ensure that all was right. In the first performance Richard was cast as a Cavalier in the Prologue, and I was a Court Lady. In the first act, Richard was one of the four princes in the famous "Rose Adagio." I was the centre girl in the "Garland Dance." We were both Courtiers in the second act and, in the third act, Richard was the Wolf with Red Riding Hood; I was Beauty with the Beast. We performed the ballet from February to June—78 consecutive performances.

Meanwhile, we were rehearsing for other ballets to be added to our repertoire, the first of which was Robert Helpmann's *Adam Zero*. Ashton's lovely *Symphonic Variations* was next. Very few company members saw any of *Symphonic Variations* until the first performance. So on that night, the wings were full of dancers watching it for the first time. I remember sitting with my good friend Rosemary Lindsay, and the two of us crying at the beauty of it and the Cesar Franck score. That first cast being Margot Fonteyn (brunette), Pamela May (blonde), Moira Shearer (redhead), Michael Somes, Brian Shaw and Henry Danton, who had been in the International Ballet with me.

Other Helpmann ballets we performed in were *Miracle in the Gorbals* and *Hamlet.* One time in *Gorbals,* during a street-fight scene, one of the stage knives that Richard was held was not covered enough, and it slightly cut his hand. It drew a little blood. Bobby, who was the central figure, immediately whispered to Richard, "Wipe it on me—wipe it on me." He loved the dramatic effect. Richard was delighted when he was cast as Laertes in Helpmann's *Hamlet.* It was a marvelous part. One time Bobby told Richard to tone it down; he evidently thought Richard was upstaging him

Helpmann was also an accomplished stage and screen actor. Two particularly memorable performances for me were his Oberon opposite Vivien Leigh as Titania in a beautiful production of *A Midsummer Night's Dream* at the Old Vic Theatre in 1938, and his portrayal of the Bishop of Ely in *King Henry V* starring Laurence Olivier—a film, which at the time, was one of the few things I would like to have with me if I were stranded on a desert island.

Adam Zero did not stay in the repertoire for long but, as with all Bobby's work, it was good theatre. But that was Bobby: a remarkable artist, a true man of the theatre both as a dancer and as an actor. Sometimes he could be a little outrageous during a performance. He would turn upstage during a dramatic scene and make a comic aside or gesture unbeknownst to the audience (but making it very hard for us to keep straight faces) and then turn around and go right back to his dramatic role. Richard always says he learned so much theatrically from working with Bobby. I think we all did, and he especially taught the company how to act—a quality that still makes the Sadler's Wells Ballet, or Royal Ballet as it is now called, stand out above other companies in the world. We were fortunate to have so many fine artists in the company and to be a part of that golden era: an era created by Ninette de Valois.

2. Ninette de Valois. Ballet Theatre.

Ninette de Valois was a truly admirable woman. What she achieved by her perseverance was nothing short of a miracle, considering those difficult early days with her small band of dancers, her association with the temperamental Lilian Baylis and on to the emergence of the Vic-Wells, then the Sadler's Wells and, finally, Royal Ballet companies. She had an incredibly ordered and brilliant mind. She choreographed most of *The Rake's Progress* while recovering in a hospital after an operation. We always said she should have been in government. She was an excellent speaker and diplomat.

Like most of us, she had her idiosyncrasies. Perhaps her best known was, if you were sitting beside her at rehearsals, if something wasn't right, she would slap your knee and say, "Sno goot my dear sno goot" (phonetically). This must have resulted in quite a few bruised knees.

Richard tells an amusing anecdote about Madam. She used to get migraine headaches. One day, a dancer in the company asked to be excused because she had a migraine. De Valois replied, "Sno goot girl, only intelligent people get migraines." She could not understand how anyone would allow pain or discomfort to stop them from doing their job. There were not many like her. She had survived the rigors of touring with the Diaghilev company and expected us to do the same. Yet she tried her best to see that we were well treated.

Richard became aware of this fact when, as our company Equity (union) representative, he attended meetings involving other English dance companies and they would be asking for better conditions. Richard had nothing to say on our account because we already had most of what the others were complaining about.

At the end of our first season at Covent Garden, America's Ballet Theatre came to the Opera House. Richard and I went to the opening-night performance. Their *Les Sylphides* did not impress us. And we had been puzzled by advance publicity at what was billed as *The Black Swan*. We were surprised when we found out it was the *pas de deux* from the third act of *Swan Lake*. We had not seen it in a black tutu before.

Blue Beard, with Irina Baronova and Anton Dolin was quite delightful. But Jerome Robbins' *Fancy Free* excited us the most. It was like no other ballet we had ever seen; the marvelous male variations thrilled us. The next day Richard and I went on holiday with my mother and Hil on the Isle of Wight in a happy mood.

Returning from our holiday, the company toured the provinces and Scotland before going back to Covent Garden, where *Giselle* and *Les Sirènes*, a new ballet by Ashton, were presented. I loved being in *Giselle* again, and *Les Sirènes* was lighthearted and the Cecil Beaton costumes were fun to wear, especially in a seaside scene with Edwardian bathing suits.

In October, the company traveled to Vienna on its first European tour since moving to Covent Garden.

3. Vienna Tour.

The following are excerpts from letters I sent to my mother while I was on tour in Vienna:

"Under the auspices of the British Council. October 1946. Train to Dover. Beautiful day and the White Cliffs looked *so* white against the blue, blue sky. It was a calm crossing—the sea was like glass. We were treated rather like troops by an army officer, as we were under the military. When we reached Calais, the men and women were separated. We went to a transit camp and were told to go to the officer's mess, where we were in with the British Army wives and bawling children, and given one small sandwich, cake and cup of tea. We were there over an hour during which time we got our money changed to Austrian currency.

"We then boarded the train. Delicious sleepers, two to a compartment. Rosemary and I are together. The bunks tip up for seats during the day and there is a window across one end of the carriage, which opens all the way down. Wash basin, a little heater and reading lamps. Almost like a little flat!

"We were installed for some time before the boys arrived. They, the dirty dogs, had been to the men's mess, had a big meal and were given drinks and then sandwiches to take with them. We were mad at them! There was a man selling grapes, so we bought some—they are so good.

"We were then given a wonderful meal on the train, beautifully cooked—even on a train. We also bought a bottle of red wine, and the bread is snowy white.

"We are nearing Metz (France). It is a pleasant country, not very flat and the trees are lovely now. Next stop was Nancy. It was a lovely day. How I adore the homes here with their quaint shapes, wrought iron balconies, their shutters and window boxes—it is *so* delicious whether it was the sun being out or not—it was all so bright.

"The next stop was Strasbourg, which looks lovely with many more individual houses.

"We are now seeing some real signs of war. It has been badly smashed and the station is very tatty.

"We have just crossed the Rhine. We are now in Germany. Here bridges are down.

"The first stop across the river looks as though this was the first train through after it was bombed—such a mess. It is wonderful all the same how they have cleared the railways. The next ports of call are Karlsruhe and then Munich. Karlsruhe was also a mess and nothing has been done to the place—it must have been a lovely town—but it really is dead. We were there for half an hour. We got out and walked through the station to the main street but there were few people about—a few were clamoring for papers, obviously wanting news of the trials. (Nuremburg)

"There were trains running but you wondered where they would go to or what they would find—there seems to be nothing but ruins.

"This AM we woke up just as we were leaving Salzburg. Oh what heaven! A glorious misty morning, with the sun a lovely pink shade shining on a huge mountain and on top of a tiny hill, rather like San Michel, was a castle—a real fairy-tale one!

"From then on the scenery was breathtaking. Can't believe I am seeing the real thing—it is like a travel talk, only we can lean out of the windows and almost touch it and smell the wonderful air. I have tried to sketch bits but it is rather hopeless—the scenery moves so fast. It is all wonderful—valleys and ravines that keep appearing from unexpected places. We are being driven by two funny little electric engines, one at each end. It is good as there are no smuts.

"I haven't seen any specially nice peasant costumes—just a few men in the usual Tyrolean garb.

"We are now on the way to Villach. We hear we are to arrive in Vienna tonight about 10:30 instead of tomorrow morning.

"We had met a young doctor, who looked Indian or Burmese. He said we should get 2 shillings a cigarette in Vienna and that there is little to buy there, but is a wonderful place to stay in.

"We keep passing 'Giselle' looking castles perched high on little mountains.

"About 8:30 we apparently got to the Russian zone and they held up the train for awhile while they boarded the train. We were given passes to show them, but they never saw me! It was about 11:30 before we reached Vienna. We were all so tired—hardly knew what was happening—except that I eventually found a bed!

"We are all divided between two transit hotels. Richard is in the famous Sachers and I am in the one next door, this naturally disappointed us. Vienna must have been wonderful before all the damage was done. Such big buildings and the streets are so wide, so much history.

"The next evening we were supposed to go to see *Tanhauser* but got lost and mistook the time so instead we sat at the hotel bar, drank and gossiped! Next day we got lost a bit again trying to find the theatre. Got there eventually and I collected my practice clothes and went back to a class with Ninette. It was first for a week—we all felt so weak. Awful! In the afternoon went shopping and bought two pairs of fully-fashioned silk stockings at the British Welfare shop. My first ever!

"We were going to see *Tosca* at the Volksoper. When we got there we were put in a box! I had hoped I might be converted to opera—but no—I think it was worse than ever—though I hear from people who know that it was not a wonderful performance. The music was lovely but oh dear—only one person could act and he couldn't sing. The theatre is very cold and bleak looking and the house was half empty. I hope it will be better for us. After the opera, we went to the Kinsky Palace—it's an amazing place. Terrific staircase and furniture, cherubs, murals and everything plush. There was a large bar at the Kinsky Palace and one shelf was designated to liqueurs, every imaginable one. So each time we went there we tried a new one—all new to me, and I discovered there and then, that Grand Marnier was my favorite!

"We had supper and I had my first champagne and liked it! Tomorrow we have a cocktail party in the morning and then we are all being taken to Shronbrun. It is so wonderful—especially the little theatre. I waltzed in the famous ballroom and knocked on the desk Napoleon knocked when he was dictating his terms for some treaty.

"We went to see some of the famous buildings but sadly the Opera House and St. Stephen's Cathedral were so badly damaged that we weren't able to go near them.

"The city was divided into three sections, British, Russian and French. Our hotels were on the corner of the British and Russian sectors. As the Russians guarded their side with soldiers with fixed bayonets we crossed carefully on the opposite side of the street.

"Many of the company had bought cigarettes, coffee, tea and soap to sell to the locals.

"Richard had set up "shop" on his dressing room table. One evening he was visited by a man in uniform, obviously top brass. Richard was slightly concerned—but the man only wanted to buy some things. So Richard sighed with relief. He afterwards found out the man was the chief of police!!

"One day we were driven to the Vienna Woods and we were able to look down on the Danube River. Unfortunately it was a dull day and it was not the Blue Danube."

4. Engagement. Marriage.

By 1946 we had added *The Rake's Progress*, *Nocturne*, *Miracle in the Gorbals*, *Les Patineurs*, *Dante Sonata*, *Les Sylphides*, *Hamlet*, *Giselle*, *Coppélia*, *Carnaval* and *Le Lac des Cygnes* to our repertoire. Most of these ballets had been in the Sadler's Wells Ballet repertoire prior to moving to Covent Garden. Many of them were created for the smaller stage and needed to be adjusted to the larger Opera House stage, and we had to learn to fill it out and to project more in order to reach the larger audiences.

Later that year, Richard and I became engaged. He had been staying with us in Ealing and proposed to me in the garden sitting on the steps outside the little wooden house my mother had someone build for me. My mother approved of Richard and so did Hil. I was very happy. Richard took me to the Burlington Arcade in London, where he bought my engagement ring, gold with garnets—my favorite. We celebrated the event with my mother, Hilary and Denis at the Pastori Hotel. In fact, we often returned there to celebrate birthdays and other special occasions. We planned to marry on Saturday, March 22, 1947. By coincidence, it was on that date eight years earlier, we both appeared at the Royal Opera House together—I as a page and Richard as a soloist in the gala performance of *The Sleeping Princess* for the French President and his wife.

The winter of 1947 was horrible; bitterly cold and damp—the worst on record. We were performing in *The Fairy Queen* by Purcell with choreography by Frederick

Ashton. It included one of his beautiful *pas de deux* danced by Margot Fonteyn and Michael Somes as "Spirits of the Air." Because the stage at the Opera House was not always free for us to rehearse, we had to go to the Chenies Street Drill Hall—a cold and uncomfortable place. So cold in fact, that one day I wore gloves for barre work. The metal barres were freezing. It was the first time the opera company had appeared at the Opera House since its reopening, *The Fairy Queen*, combining the ballet and opera, was based on Shakespeare's *A Midsummer Night's Dream*. Robert Helpmann played Oberon; Margaret Rawlings Titania. I was one of six fairy attendants to Titania, and we were costumed in flimsy dresses, not suitable for the bone-chilling cold in the theatre. Some nights the audience brought blankets to keep themselves warm.

In one scene, the fairies had to sit around a fountain that sprayed us with real, ice-cold water. It was miserable. One of the male dancers portraying the Sun King sat on a raised throne not moving. So he hid a hot water bottle inside his breast plate to keep warm.

I had hoped to save my mother some money by having my wedding bouquet made up of spring flowers from our garden. But the weather was so bad, there were no flowers out. My poor mother had to send to the Scily Isles for the spring flowers, costing her a lot of money. Added to this problem, Richard had booked rooms for our two-day honeymoon at the charming hotel, The Bell at Hurley on the Thames (nicknamed the "Hell at Burley"). But two days before our wedding, the hotel phoned to say it had rained so much they were flooded and had to cancel all bookings. A friend of Denis' came to the rescue and booked us into a very nice hotel near them in Aylesbury. We had only two days because we had to be back to work on Tuesday.

Our wedding was held at St. Matthew's Church on Ealing Common, a short distance from where I was born. My father gave me away; Denis was Richard's best man; my little cousin, Jane Bond, was my bridesmaid; friends and family also attended, Leslie Edward and Michael Somes were ushers. Margot Fonteyn, Pamela May, Harold Turner and his wife Gerd Larsen, and Frederick Ashton attended the service, but had to leave directly afterwards because they had to get back to the theatre for a performance. We still have some of the lovely gifts they gave us: engraved crystal goblets from Margot, a Wedgewood vase from Pamela, and a set of Bristol blue glasses and decanters from Fred.

After we were pronounced man and wife and started our walk down the aisle, Fred loudly announced, "Slower, slower," still giving us instructions. Luckily the weather had improved slightly. It was dull, with a few sprinkles of rain, but they say a little rain on your wedding day brings good luck.

Richard and I lived in his tiny flat in Bina Gardens for about three months after we were married. Then we found a nice flat at 10 Devonshire Terrace near Lancaster Gate, where we lived until we left for America. It was one floor up, with a bedroom, living room, dining room, bathroom and kitchen, from which we could walk out onto a roof where we put a few window boxes.

We decorated the flat with some of our combined belongings and some things that Denis gave us. In the dining room we were able to use the six mahogany chairs from Sally Park, which my mother had given us. They were Adam-style chairs made in the 18th century, with the Handcock crest inlaid in the backs. As in most homes in England in those days, there were no refrigerators. Most had little pantries in as cool a place as possible and, if necessary, we would go to the fishmongers for a slab of ice to keep butter and milk fresh.

While we were on Devonshire Terrace, Freddie Franklin came from America to visit friends and family. He stayed in a hotel in Lancaster Gate near us.

I couldn't believe I was finally going to meet him. Richard had told me of their friendship when we first met. Freddie came to see us as soon as he arrived in London and presented us with two enormous steaks (about six months meat ration). We were stunned. They were so big, we had trouble cooking them on our tiny gas grill. It was such a delight to meet him after all those years of adoration.

Just before Fred's visit, Richard had bought a secondhand car for 100 pounds. It was an SSI—the prototype of the Jaguar, with a very long bonnet (hood), huge headlights and it smoked like a chimney. We think it used up more oil than gas. We drove Freddie to his hotel one evening, and he said he couldn't see us leave because of all the smoke. One day near Buckingham Palace, a Rolls drew up beside us, and the chauffeur looked at us and held his nose. We didn't care. It had four wheels and got us around. Richard finally got rid of it, selling it for 100 pounds. But before doing so, he stuffed a raw potato in the exhaust pipe.

5. Léonide Massine.

In 1947, de Valois invited the famous Léonide Massine to stage some of his ballets for the company. The first was *The Three-Cornered Hat,* or *Tricorne,* as we called it.

Massine was fascinating to work for, but quite the task master. It's been thought that, because of the long hours he used to rehearse, dancers formed their union to limit the length of rehearsal times. Even so, as Equity representative for our company, Richard had to say to Massine on more than one occasion that his time was up, or he would have gone on and on.

Massine always came to rehearsals with his "little black book" for reference purposes. Most of us loved *Tricorne* for its uniqueness. Some of us went to a Spanish dance teacher to help us with the style Massine wanted. I enjoyed my costume, with its distinctive broad-brimmed hat.

We were all amazed that Massine still performed his own role of the Miller, an exhausting part (as were all the solos he created for himself). During his solo, he used to mutter some undistinguishable sounds as he slapped his thighs. Later, when Harold Turner took on the role of the Miller, he thought it might help if he made some sounds, too. So he used to mutter his phone number—Hampstead two-three-six, or whatever.

After *Tricorne*, Massine produced *La Boutique Fantasque*, which most of us did not enjoy, except for watching Massine dance his original role in the "Can-Can."

For our summer holiday, we traveled to Ireland and visited friends in Cork and some of my old haunts.

On our return to work, we spent days rehearsing with Massine, who gave us lots of seemingly disjointed sequences of steps. They were fussy and intricate; we weren't sure what they were all about. Meanwhile, Massine also was working on *The Red Shoes* film in which he had a major role. When the reviews for the film came out, some erroneously stated that in addition to the stars Moira Shearer, Léonide Massine and Robert Helpmann, the Sadler's Wells Ballet was in it. Not so. The truth is there were a few dancers from the company; the others were "pick-up" dancers, some of whom joined the company later. Finally, de Valois came into one of Massine's rehearsals at Sadler's Wells and explained the ballet he was teaching us: It was *Mam'zelle Angot*, which also had been set on America's Ballet Theatre. We liked *Angot*, especially the ballroom scene, and Richard had the good role of the Officer.

Clock Symphony, Massine's third ballet for the company, was not a great success. We remember, though, while on a tour of England and appearing at a theatre with a deeply raked stage, at one moment in *Clock Symphony,* part of the set began to move downstage. So Richard and John Field, both in the cast, had to rush behind the gazebo and hold onto it to stop it from rolling any farther.

Another not-so-successful ballet that season was Ashton's *Don Juan*. Richard had the role of the husband to Moira Shearer's wife. During one of the early performances, Moira swore at Richard during their *pas de deux*. He, in return replied to her that if she swore at him again, he would drop her on her ___! From then, they got on very well. De Valois revived her famous ballet *Job*, with Robert Helpmann as Satan. When Anton Dolin came as guest artist later in the year, he needed someone to "paint" the ribs on his body before each performance. Being an artist, I volunteered—a fun experience.

The last production that year was Ashton's first three-act ballet, *Cinderella*. Sadly, Margot was injured and unable to do the first performance. But Moira was lovely in the title role. Ashton and Helpmann were unforgettable as The Ugly Sisters. I played one of the Stars and, as always, enjoyed working with Fred. His lovely ballet, *Nocturne,* was revived that year and, happily, I was in the cast. It was always a favorite of mine, with the atmospheric music, *Paris—A Song of a Great City* by Delius.

Richard also was cast in *Nocturne* and sometimes replaced Ashton in his role of the Spectator. For a long time, Richard was the only person to do so.

For a while, the company ballet master was Harijus Plucis, a Latvian who had been the leading male dancer at the Riga National Opera. We went to daily company classes most of the time. I found Plucis helpful, as he made me aware of "pulling up" more, and he assisted me with my pirouettes. Otherwise, I was not altogether happy with his classes. Many of the company members and I would go as often as possible to Vera

Volkova, a wonderful teacher who had studied with the famous Agrippina Vaganova in Russia. Vera's classes were always very well attended, but the studio on West Street in London was not very large. We used to say you had to have been well turned out in second position, as often we were packed like sardines at the barre.

6. European Tours, 1947-1948.

In September 1947, the company was off on a six-week European tour. These are the impressions I wrote to my mother.

"On our way to Brussels from Ostend, we were amazed at how well the land had recovered from the war, every scrap had been tilled and, even at 6:30 in the evening, the fields were full of people working—not like in England where they would have stopped work by then. There were lots of new houses even in the short distance we traveled, more than we had ever seen in England. A lesson in how to recover!"

BRUSSELS. Theatre Royal de la Monnaie. September 10-11.

"We were met in Brussels by Denis. At that time he was working at the British Embassy in Paris. We stayed in a hotel on the Place de Bruckère. The weather was lovely. We were thrilled with all the city lights and so much in all the shops. Richard and I were so happy to be together on this tour—our first as husband and wife.

"We met a mutual friend of Denis and Leslie's, named Lucien. He was a dear and gave some of us a wonderful party.

"On the way to Prague, we stopped in Paris. Denis had already returned there, and met us at the station and took us to the Embassy for lunch. As he had to go back to work, we went on a short tour—up the Eiffel Tower—Paris looked wonderful, it was a beautiful day. We also went along the Champs Elysées and had a look at the Opera House. Two capitals in one day!

The train trip to Prague was through Germany, but it was night time."

PRAGUE. Velka Opera. September 15-21.

"Very nice theatre—huge rehearsal room. I remember Ninette giving us a one-hour barre!!

"Nancy Wake, Denis' compatriot in SOE in France, was in Prague and we were able to meet her which was good.

"But the city was very sinister, especially in the hotel—we felt any moment we would have a knife in our backs. All very depressing—and the heat was awful and oppressive. We were in the low part of the city. On the other side of the river, the city was rather nice and high up. We were taken there one day on a guided tour. We went to two castles, one which has St. Vitus Cathedral in it. Magnificent stained glass—breathtaking colors. The church itself was very simple which showed off the windows so well. Food was bad and we were hungry.

"We went to quite a few "dos." British Council, British Embassy and the theatre all entertained us. Apparently, the company was a terrific success in Prague, as announced on BBC.

One night we went to a Hungarian night club. There were so many of us we completely took over the place. The band was wonderful."

WARSAW. Teatr Polski. September 25-29.

"On the train to Warsaw, we had breakfast. It was one of the first good meals we had had since before Prague.

"Soon we were told we were nearing Warsaw and soon the train stopped and we were told we had arrived. But there was nothing there—hardly a platform—no station. It looked like the end of the world.

"We were met by Leon Woizikowsky, who had been in Warsaw all through the war. He was so happy to see Ninette and she him. Dear man.

"We had never seen such damage, it really was tragic. Fortunately, it was a little cooler - we had not been prepared for the heat we had had during the last two weeks. A very nice guide took us on a bus tour of Warsaw—he had been through all the horrors. We were taken first to the old part of town—the city center. We thought it was the end of everything—so sad. It must have been a lovely place as one could see from the remains of some buildings. There were many parks and avenues.

"Then we went to the Ghetto, which was just too ghastly for words, all that was left was the remnants of the wall which had been built around the Ghetto. But despite all the terrible damage, we found the atmosphere far nicer than Prague. As we went about the city we saw so many poor people with wheel barrows or whatever collecting bricks or anything they could to help rebuild their city.

"How remarkable it was that the theatre was one of the first places to be rebuilt. On the first night we could hardly get onstage—the wings were full—there were people everywhere hanging on to anything they could to see the ballet. The audience were so thrilled to see ballet again (we were the first company to perform in Warsaw after the war). They clapped in time all the way through most of the ballets. Very moving. It made dancing so worthwhile. We did seven performances in four days. Two of the shows were extra in aid of the reconstruction of the city.

"We were entertained every day by someone or another, always wonderful food—salmon, eggs, borsht, sour cream and cakes. It made us feel so guilty."

POZNAN. Teatr Wielki. October 1-5

"A nice little town. It was good to see shops again, but things were very expensive—how can the natives afford them?

"We were well received in a nice theatre. We were housed in a mediocre building and dined all together in a large room at a long table. Each one was given a plate of the daily staple of ham and eggs and bread and in this case, a pickle as well. Most of us did not want them but one girl liked them, so one by one we handed our pickles to her until her plate was piled high!

"One day the 'stars' were invited to a special breakfast hosted by the city's high officials. When they were seated, they found there was a full glass of Polish Slivovitz at each place and it was evidently protocol to drink it and more. Well most of the "stars" arrived back at the theatre just a little drunk and we had a matinée to perform! All we could do was ply them with lots of black coffee and hope for the best!

"Talking of drinks, one of the theatres on this tour had a full bar on the dressing room level. Not a good idea!

"The train ride to Danzig on our way to Sweden was uncomfortable—all the seats were wooden and the coaches badly lit.

"In Danzig harbour we saw the remains of sunken German battleships.

"We had breakfast before boarding the ship to take us to Malmo. I remember having raw eggs—that was a first! Unfortunately, Richard was not well—in fact there were three invalids on the trip to Malmo."

MALMO. Stadsteater. October 12-14

"It was lovely to see lights in the streets and shops again. Malmo is a lovely place—but we resented the smugness of most of the Swedes after Poland's devastation. Richard was better but not dancing. The theatre was large and modern."

OSLO. National Theatre. October 16-19

"Very beautiful, especially the surroundings. I went for my first plane ride (and I'm an R.A.F. pilot's daughter!) in a small plane flying over part of the Oslo fjord."

In March 1948, the company returned to Holland—to The Hague, Amsterdam and Rotterdam.

Richard found it strange going back to The Hague, with memories of the ordeal there in 1940. He had described the hotel to me as spacious with a wide staircase. On returning, it suddenly appeared quite small. Time can play tricks with one's mind. We loved Amsterdam and took a few guided tours of the canals and to the docks.

One funny incident happened in our hotel there. Being married, Richard and I usually got a larger room than most in the company. So our room was often the place to party. At a last-night get together in our room in Amsterdam, our bed collapsed from all the people sitting on it. We managed to prop it up with beer bottles. This worked, but we were terrified that the hotel would find out before we left. We couldn't get out soon enough. Luckily, we never heard a word from the hotel.

Then in October, the company went on a tour to Paris at the Théâtre des Champs Elysées. One evening, Richard said he was going to take me out to dinner somewhere special. So we walked along the Champs Elysées until we reached Fouquets, the famous restaurant. To my surprise, we went in and enjoyed a wonderful dinner. Then Richard told me that when he was in Paris, with the company in 1937, he had passed Fouquets and swore he would return to eat there. So here we were sharing a very special evening.

On to Düsseldorf and Hamburg. In Düsseldorf during a half-day off, a group of us took a bus tour to Cologne and its surroundings. Richard's back had been bothering him for a while, and the bus ride really aggravated the pain. That evening, while performing *Dante Sonata*, the first ballet on the program, Richard suffered an injury. At one moment Pamela May, lying prone on the stage, had to be lifted arm's length over Richard's head. He reached down to lift her and felt a dreadful pain in his back. Frantically, he whispered to Pamela that his back had gone out. Somehow he got through the rest of the ballet and, even worse, through the demanding *Les Patineurs* and *Checkmate*. Afterwards, we returned to the hotel and he went to bed. Richard awoke in the morning and said he felt paralyzed.

I called Herbert (Bertie) Hughes, our company manager, who said that Richard would have to be flown back to London as soon as possible. Meanwhile the company was leaving by bus that day for Hamburg. So the company arranged for Richard to travel by car to Hamburg and, from there, by plane to London. Richard was as comfortable as could be lying flat in the front seat of a chauffeur-driven, super-charged Mercedes-Benz. I sat in the back. We tore along the Autobahn at an alarming speed. Richard said he had visions of flying through the windshield feet first.

We got to Hamburg, which was a horrible sight, such devastation. Richard was flown back to London and to St. Bartholomew's Hospital, where he stayed for three weeks lying on a board for what turned out to be a slipped disc. So he always says it's like a title to a song, "I slipped my disc in Düsseldorf."

Fortunately, for me, the tour ended in Hamburg. So within a couple of days, I was back home and able to visit Richard in hospital until his release. He still had to sleep on a board for a while.

7. Alexandra Danilova and Frederic Franklin.
Holiday in France. Vaslav Nijinsky.

Alexandra Danilova and Frederic Franklin appeared as guest artists with the Sadler's Wells Ballet in March 1948—a thrill to see our friend Fred again and to experience Danilova and Massine dancing together in their original roles as the "Can-Can" dancers in *La Boutique Fantasque*. Someone worked out that their combined ages came to over 100 years. Unfortunately, Danilova injured her foot and was unable to dance Swanilda in *Coppélia,* as scheduled, with Fred as Franz. So Moira Shearer took her place for a couple of performances. We remember Fred being so delighted to work with her. Even though Danilova was not performing due to her injury, she did manage to give the company girls a pointe class, which was a pleasure for us.

In June 1948, Richard and I planned a holiday with Denis. In Paris we slept on the floor of Denis' flat. The next morning, the three of us boarded a bus for Marseilles. During the bus ride, Denis often remarked, "Oh, there's a prison that I was in for a while" or "there's a field I landed in"—referring to his days in Special Operations Executive.

Our destination was Sanary, a small town on the coast of the South of France between Marseilles and Toulon. We all stayed in a nice little pension run by a lady we nicknamed "Madame tout-suite," as she always said "tout-suite" to everything.

Fortunately, Denis was able to borrow the local chemist's car for a couple of days. We wanted to get to Cannes, as Fred Franklin was there on holiday, and Denis wanted to attend a ball being held there with some famous people he knew. With Richard driving, we eventually got to Cannes—quite a distance from Sanary.

We met Freddie and Leon Danielian on the terrace of the Carlton Hotel on the Croisette in Cannes. We sat and talked for ages. One of the hotel staff came up to Denis and said, "I know you." Denis said, "Yes, I remember you." Evidently, during the German occupation of France—Denis, as a radio operator for the underground movement—was working secretly in a room at the top of the Carlton. Denis then started to relate some of his war escapades. Freddie and Leon were fascinated—their jaws dropping in amazement at the things Denis had done.

In the evening we went with Freddie and Leon to a bar on the Croisette, and they were playing a record of Edith Piaf singing *La Vie en Rose*. It has special meaning for me now. Freddie asked us to join him and some of the other dancers from the Ballet Russe de Monte Carlo to spend the day in Monte Carlo. It was a happy day spent mostly in the swimming pool. Fred then gave us an interesting tour of the Opera House, where he had performed with the company.

The next day we had to return the car to Sanary. We hated leaving our friends and that part of the world, which is so beautiful and glamorous, especially seeing it for the first time.

It must have been sometime in 1949 that the company was informed Vaslav Nijinsky was going to be attending the evening performance. This caused quite a stir. We were at Covent Garden and, during the ballet, we tried to see him as he sat in the Staff box, where Madam watched many performances.

After the performance, we were asked to remain on stage. Nijinsky was to come and meet us. But it was a sad meeting. The man who had been such a great artist and legend walked on stage, supported by his wife Romola. A nondescript man, he stood amongst us staring blankly and, when we applauded him, he weakly flapped his hands about—not the way we would have wished to see the great Nijinsky. It was depressing and, sometime later, we heard about his death.

8. Frederick Ashton.

In 1949 Ashton revived *Apparitions*, which was a delight. The dramatic Liszt music, the beautiful Beaton costumes and, for once, Fred allowed Richard and me to be partners. Usually he disliked married couples dancing together because he said they always fought.

Ashton's ballets were a joy to be in, and how happy I was to be cast in most of them. I loved working with Fred and admired his exquisite taste, his love of romanticism, his musicality (though he could not read a score), his range—from abstract to comedy to tragedy—and his genius in conveying emotions. His special use of *port de bras* and *épaulement* have become symbols of the Royal Ballet.

Fred used to get very involved with his cast at rehearsals for a new ballet, drawing ideas from their interpretations of what he gave them to do or ideas they might offer to help with his main theme. It was always exciting being in on the early stages of one of his creations.

While choreographing *Daphnis and Chloë*, a group of us girls waited around—some sitting on the floor back to back; some lying down. Fred spotted us and told us to remember our positions. We apparently looked like a Greek frieze, which he liked and then incorporated into the first part of the ballet.

9. Florence Tour. Villa at Cap Ferrat.

In May 1949, the Sadler's Wells Ballet participated in the Maggio Musicale in Florence, Italy. We performed at the Teatro Communale from May 20 to 30.

From letters to my mother :

"The scenery was lovely as we went around Lake Geneva. I saw Chillon Castle (Granny's castle in her painting). We then went through the famous Simplon Tunnel, but our journey to Florence was uncomfortable as we sat on the train from 2 p.m. on Sunday until 10:30 a.m. on Monday, with the exception of three hours stop in Milan, where we hurriedly went to the famous arcade and a quick visit to La Scala Theatre.

"Florence was heavenly. Since we were not performing every night, we had a chance to see some of the magnificent sights.

"On one evening off, we went to Gluck's *Orpheo*—not one of our favorites. Richard and I left after two acts, but we were sitting near Princess Margaret's box. She looked lovely, and we saw her again when she attended the ballet.

"We had one whole day off, and some of the company opted to go to Rome. But Richard and I and some of the other dancers decided we didn't want to see Rome in one short day. So we took a trip into the beautiful mountains above Florence and visited the little town of Fiesole, with its breathtaking view of the city below. We saw the remains of a Roman theatre there. It's quite marvelous how much has been preserved and still being used for performances.

"Another day, a small group of us decided to visit Pisa. We took a local bus, which dropped us off at the Piazza del Duomo. From there, we climbed the famous Leaning Tower—a rather weird sensation due to its odd incline. On reaching the top, we enjoyed the views and climbed further to the bell chamber. On seeing the bell, Richard and one other boy decided to ring it. No sooner done, than a couple of guards came hurrying up and reprimanded them. The bell was rung only on special occasions, and this was not one of them. So we all descended back to the Piazza and crossed over to the Duomo. We looked inside. When we came out we relaxed on the steps. Because it was a sweltering day, we girls pulled our skirts up over our knees. Again a couple of *polizia* appeared and reprimanded us—this time for corrupting the minds of the bambinos. We got the feeling we were not welcome in Pisa and soon got ourselves back to Florence."

In July 1949, Richard and I returned to France for our holiday. At that time, there were still travel restrictions for regular tourists going abroad. One was allowed only a small amount of money to carry—hardly sufficient to pay for any length of time. But there was a system whereby one could get around this. It was called Autocheques. You were able to rent a car, go each day to a listed hotel with breakfast included—all paid for in advance before leaving England. We used this method quite successfully.

Dancers Rosemary Lindsay and Dorothea (Dolly) Zaymes joined us. Richard was the only driver and drove us to Dover, where we and the car were put onto the ferry. On reaching Calais, we unloaded and were on our way to Beaulieu, near Nice and Cap Ferrat on the Riviera. We made a couple of overnight stops at listed hotels. The only difficulty was when we had to phone ahead for accommodations for the four of us. My French was not that good, especially trying to understand some of the fast talking telephone operators. But we managed, and all went well.

While making our way from Sisteron up through the Route Napoléon, something went wrong with the car. We were almost above the tree line, and it was very hot. A man in a sports car drove by, never stopping to help. All he did was thumb his nose. Then a truck came by and a man got out and examined the car. He spoke French, but we managed to understand there was a part that had to be replaced, necessitating Richard to go with him to the next town to get it. So off Richard went with a complete stranger, leaving us three girls alone with the car in the baking sun. Since the car was in the sun, I very nervously managed to reverse it into the shade. It was a scary time, as we had no idea where Richard had gone or how long he would be away.

Eventually about an hour later, the truck returned with Richard and the man, who happily fixed whatever ailed the car. we were on our way again, climbing higher and higher until we started the descent on our way to Grasse. To our surprise, we came upon the man in the sports car. He was in trouble this time, but we treated him as he had us and continued on our way.

When arrived in Beaulieu, we got in touch with Michael Somes as previously planned. He and Jean Gilbert, the company pianist, were staying with a friend at a villa on Cap Ferrat, and they invited us over. The villa was fantastic—a tall Italianate building that stood out like a landmark. The entranceway was made of Italian tiles; and statues and balustrades encircled the garden.

An enormous room, with very high ceilings and heavy furnishing on the main floor, looked like an opera set. The large windows opened out onto a balcony, overlooked the sea to nearby Monte Carlo and the spectacular background of the mountains. Up a large staircase, we came to a modern suite. Then an elevator took us to another floor, which housed a complete apothecary's shop.

On the top floor there was a large bedroom, with a huge four-poster bed that David insisted on using, and a sinister-looking sarcophagus.

David Copley Thaw was Michael's and Jean's American friend. His mother, we were told, had been a friend of old man Singer (of sewing machine fame) who, according to legend, had built the villa for his-then lover Isadora Duncan. David had full use of the villa. He was a delightful young man and an aspiring and talented singer.

We spent every day at the villa. One day, Jean was playing the piano by the window, open to the balcony where David stood and sang arias—what a setting! The rest of us were lying around in the sun by the pool—the pool actually a small harbor between the villa and the one opposite, which belonged to Somerset Maugham.

We also made some time to drive around and sightsee. We drove on the Grande Corniche, quite scary. We saw the villa, which had been used in the film *The Red Shoes,* when Moira Shearer ran up the long flight of steps to the villa entrance. We visited Monte Carlo and, at the station, Dolly simulated Moira's character's "death" by standing on the station bridge.

Another day we went to St. Jean Cap Ferrat, where we sat on a low roadside wall and watched the Tour de France cyclists as they sped by. We returned to work looking very tanned. For *Les Sylphides*, I had to use a lot of wet-white to cover the tan.

Here are (left to right) Fiorella Keane, Julia Farron, Gillian Lynn, Christine Du Boulay and Nadia Nerina.

Ballet Off to USA

At Yuma station: Leslie Edwards, Frederick Ashton, Richard, Brian Shaw, Gillian Lynne, Pamela May, Robert Irving, Nadia Nerina, Alexander Grant.

With Moira Shearer (standing: Valerie Taylor, Pauline Wadsworth).

At Warner Bros. Studio: Leslie Edwards, Greta Hamby, Kenneth MacMillan, Doris Day, Douglas Stuart, Dorothea Zaymes, Richard.

At Zuma beach: Peter Clegg, Pauline Wadsworth, Angela Walton, myself, Oscar Berlin.

In *Dante Sonata*. Photo: Maurice Seymour.

above:
Richard in *Les Patineurs* (Pas de Deux).
Photo: Maurice Seymour.

right:
In *Ballet Imperial*.
Photo: Roger Wood.

Chapter IV
First American Tour: 1949-1950

1. Preparations For The Tour.

After our holiday in France, we performed in and around London from August to September and prepared for our first visit to America. Richard was excited at the prospect of going to America, feeling half-American and having seen many American films, particularly westerns and musicals. He couldn't wait to see the real thing.

The girls in the company were given a complete wardrobe of clothes supplied by some of the best English fashion houses for publicity purposes. This included a daytime outfit with shoes, hat and gloves, a coat and a cocktail outfit with appropriate shoes. We then modeled the clothes for a series of photo sessions. It was tiring but exciting.

The boys were a bit upset since they didn't get anything. I wish to note that, in our ballet world, the men and women were always called boys and girls—no matter what age.

Richard was busy in the role of the company's Equity representative, and he was involved with the cross-Atlantic negotiations with AGMA, the American equivalent of Equity, particularly the issue of the huge discrepancy between our salaries and those of the American dancers. Things got more complicated when, the day before we left, the English government devalued the pound.

After a few days in New York, we complained about the bad food in the company's hotel. So we were all given a food allowance, which enabled us to eat anywhere.

Prior to leaving for the States, Richard and I did some research on Richard's American-born mother. We started by going to Somerset House, where most births, marriages and deaths are recorded. We eventually found Richards' parent's wedding certificate and, most amazingly, his grandparent's wedding certificate and discovered they were married by a Rev. William Du Boulay. His name is on our family tree. Destiny.

Finally, the day of our departure for New York arrived. Richard had been having more back trouble, but nothing was going to stop him from going to the States. So it was a case of grin and bear it.

On October 3rd, we arrived at London airport, where we waited hours for take off. We finally departed close to 11 p.m. Our plane, a Flying Fortress, had been converted into a commercial plane and the bomb-bay made into a bar. We had to land in Iceland and Canada to re-fuel. Ironically, my mother was reading Nevil Shute's *The Point of No Return*, a novel about a plane flying over the Atlantic and having trouble in mid-journey. Fortunately, we had no trouble, but arriving at La Guardia Airport in New York was scary, with the landing so close to the water.

Freddie Franklin was on tour, so he kindly lent Richard and me his apartment on Lexington Avenue while the rest of the company stayed in a hotel.

We rehearsed the next day at the old Metropolitan Opera House, where we were to perform. It had lots of atmosphere, even if a little dilapidated. Our final dress rehearsal of *The Sleeping Beauty* quite depressing. But, as the saying goes, "bad rehearsal, good performance."

Freddie joined us for drinks. He was on a brief break in his tour. I think he was more nervous than we were.

2. Opening Night at Metropolitan Opera House, New York.

Sunday, October 9th—the big day! We had to dress up, as there was to be a reception after the performance. Not since my wedding day had I been so nervous.

The Prologue of *The Sleeping Beauty* went extremely well. From the time the curtain went up, the audience was enthralled and enthusiastic. Freddie, Alexandra Danilova, Alicia Markova and their friend Joe Cross sat in the front row. My "stepmother" Jane was there, too, with Gertrude Lawrence's husband, Richard Aldrich.

We were chiefly concerned about how Margot would be received. We knew how marvelous she was. But would Moira's world recognition for her starring role in *The Red Shoes* overshadow Margot's unique qualities?

To add to our worries, the "Garland Dance" in Act I turned out to be a disaster. Some of the wool, which Leslie Edwards (as Catalabutte the Master of Ceremonies) snatched from the Knitting Women and threw into the wings, got caught on one of our garlands just as we were going on stage. It continued to get tangled in other garlands as the dance progressed. I was the centre turning girl and could hear some of the girls crying in despair. Finally, the nightmare ended, and we sat down in our places upstage. Margot's entrance was thrilling, helping to allay our fears. She then did a wonderful "Rose Adagio" (Richard was one of the four princes). Her performance amazed all of us. She had never been so heavenly in our eyes. There was thunderous and lengthy applause, so much so that Constant Lambert sat down in the orchestra pit while Margot and the four princes continued to take call after call.

All continued to go well, and the "Pas de Deux" in Act III again stopped the show. Margot was divine. How wonderful that Richard and I were part of that historic occasion, perhaps the most thrilling of our lives.

Following the performance, the company waited in two buses until Margot and Bobby Helpmann were ready. Then, led by a police escort with sirens blaring, we were driven to Gracie Mansion (the Mayor's official residence) to an impressive reception hosted by Mayor O'Dwyer. Gracie Mansion was a beautiful house by the river. We dined on lobster mornay and champagne served in the garden on this warm moonlit evening. A perfect finale to the day.

There were at least 300 guests at the supper, many of whom were dignitaries. As rarely happened, everyone rose and cheered Margot as she made her entrance. It was indeed Margot's night that established her as a *prima ballerina assoluta*—England's greatest, and I don't believe there will ever be another like her. The next day, the critics unanimously praised Margot and her many virtues. They gave the company and de Valois high praise. As Mayor O'Dwyer, sitting in a box with deValois, said, "Lady, you're in!"

An anecdote about that evening was told to us years later by our dear friend, the late Robert Joffrey. He related how he and Gerald Arpino had rented tuxedos, boarded one of our buses and crashed the party.

3. Margot Fonteyn.

To us, the members of the company, Margot epitomized what it meant to be a ballerina—no tantrums or temperamental airs. Everyone, including the stage staff, adored and admired her. Her warm smile and laugh made one feel at ease, even if one was in awe. When we toured, de Valois insisted we look our best. Margot certainly set a standard for us. Of course she could afford lovely clothes, but she was always so chic and knew how to wear beautiful attires. Dior discovered this and created special clothes for her.

She was a tireless worker, often putting us to shame—always doing an extra barre-work before her performance and practicing the *pas de deux* she was going to perform, especially the "Rose Adagio." She insisted on the four princes being there to help her, though on many occasions, they felt there was no need to be there when she held her balances so long. She could hold these balances on stage, too, but never to the point of being unmusical. She never resorted to flashy displays or tricks. Everything appeared unaffected and effortless. She may not have exhibited the very high extensions, multiple pirouettes and high elevation expected of most dancers these days. But she was in such control of what she was doing musically, technically and artistically—all a means to an end that allowed her to completely immerse herself in whatever role she was portraying. She was also a wonderful an intelligent actress. With her beautifully set head, huge expressive eyes, perfect back, proportioned body and impeccable line, she was a joy to watch.

We didn't see her so much once we settled in the States, and missed the ecstatic receptions she and Rudolph Nureyev experienced for their appearance at Covent Garden and around the world. We did see them together in Chicago in *Romeo and Juliet, Giselle* and a ballet Roland Petit choreographed for them.

We missed her marriage, though we did meet Roberto (Tito) Arias before their marriage and again after the tragedy of his being paralyzed from an assassination attempt.

Fortunately, there are countless films of her and books that have captured some of her perfection. She also narrated the classic television series, *The Magic of the Dance.*

4. More New York. Danny Kaye.

During our visit to New York, we were able to see some Broadway shows—*High Button Shoes, Kiss Me Kate* and Radio City. We wanted to see *South Pacific*, but it was so popular we couldn't get tickets. We heard that as we were doing equal business, the Sadler's Wells Ballet was being dubbed "North Atlantic".

After our second performance, we attended a reception at the New York Public Library, where de Valois spoke. Quite a few well-known dancers were there: Ruth Page, Vera Nemchinova, George Balanchine, Maria Tallchief, Igor Youskevitch, John Kriza, Mia Slavenska. Fred Franklin attended, too.

Our first impressions of New York were that Broadway was too flashy in more ways than one. We enjoyed seeing more color in the clothes than we were used to, and for that reason we had a fun time shopping in the many stores for items that were new or different. One item most of us girls were thrilled to be able to buy were tights. Up until our visit to America, we had only been able to afford cotton tights, which were heavy and, by the end of a performance, not fitting or baggy at the knees—we were forever pulling them up. But in New York, we found fishnet tights that stayed fitting and made our legs look so much better. It was heaven, except for the boys who complained that they got grazed necks and shoulders when lifting or lowering their partners from shoulder lifts or the like. Later we were able to buy smooth stretch tights, so everyone was pleased. Gone were our "soft furnishings," as we used to call our old tights.

We had been told that we must go to a drugstore, where we ordered a pot of tea. To our horror, we were served two cups of lukewarm water with a tea bag on the side. We thought, "What heathen land are we in?"

One day in the theatre, we heard that Danny Kaye would be visiting Bobby Helpmann. When we went down for Act I of *The Sleeping Beauty*, he was standing in the wings. One of the girls sent him a note asking him to come and see us. Bobby brought him to our dressing room, and he stayed for about ten minutes. He was sweet and amusing, as expected.

Soon after we arrived in New York, we met an ex-dancer who recommended Richard to a doctor who could help his back injury. He was able to relieve the pain a little.

We had a scare one evening. We were going to friends for dinner. When we got to their door, Richard said he needed cigarettes. When he returned, Richard said he had been knocked down by a taxi because he instinctively looked right instead of left. Fortunately, he was only slightly bruised and shaken. The taxi had bumped him, so he just let himself go and rolled over, the wheels just missing his head. Thank goodness I wasn't there, or I would have shaken for hours.

John Field (whose wife was in England), Anne Heaton, Richard and I became a regular foursome on that tour. We were invited to many events. Some were not so good, offering only meager fare when we were starving after a performance. So the four of us would politely say "goodbye." There is a fun anecdote about John, who often partnered Beryl Grey in *Le Lac des Cygnes*. John was tall, and Beryl needed tall partners whenever possible. She was beautifully proportioned but quite tall. We affectionately called her our jumbo ballerina. One day John Anne, Richard and I went across the road from the old Met stage door to the restaurant for a bite before the evening performance of *Lac*. Beryl was in the restaurant, too, tucking into a large steak and potatoes. John turned to us and said, "Oh my God, I have to lift all of that in an hour!"

When we returned to London, one evening after a performance at the Royal Opera House, I was on in the last ballet and Richard and John were not. May I say that this situation seemed to happen rather often. So they went across the road from the stage door to our favorite haunt, the famous Nag's Head, for a snack and drinks. When I was dressed and ready, I went over to join them and, to my surprise, found John's wife there, too. She immediately berated me for aiding and abetting in Anne and John's affair. She then slapped me in the face. I was certainly shocked; poor John was embarrassed. He later divorced her and married Anne. On one of our visits to London from Chicago, we went to see them at their home. John was director of the Sadler's Wells Theatre Ballet at that time. It was good to see them again.

One event that we didn't walk out on was given by J. Alden Talbot, who had invited the company for the whole day to his beautiful home in New Jersey. We were taken by bus through the Holland Tunnel across the river with a police escort to the estate. We had lunch on a lovely terrace by a lake. It was a perfect haven, and we appreciated not being herded around for once. On our return, we enjoyed the magnificent view of Manhattan with all the lights.

Another glamorous event was given by friends of Fred's at the Sherry Netherland Hotel—a superb party.

We saw Danny Kaye again at the theatre. Luckily he did not see the performance, as *Hamlet* was a disaster that night. Constant Lambert was one of the greatest ballet conductors, but prone to the bottle. On this occasion, he must have blacked out for a moment just after the opening of the ballet, because there was a long pause before the entrance of the girls, followed by some ghastly sounds from the orchestra as though all the instruments were playing something different. But we just plunged ahead and hoped for the best. Then one whole section got cut. Apparently, Bobby Helpmann had unsuccessfully tried to have the curtain lowered. It was a nightmare.

On hearing about this later, Danny Kaye, who was talking to Richard and Bobby, recounted the time when the band playing for him was all drunk, except the conductor. He was so funny impersonating a drunk saxophonist. Other stars we met were Henry Fonda, Burgess Meredith and Basil Rathbone.

Joe Cross, a friend of Freddie Franklin's, entertained us so generously, taking us to the Ritz-Carlton Oval Room and the Plaza Rendezvous Room (which had been decorated by Cecil Beaton). He also took us to the New Yorker Hotel to see John Kriza and Ruth Ann Koesun in *Salute to Cole Porter*. They were so good. Ruth Ann's husband, Eric Braun, was there too and we all sat and talked for a while. Joe then took us to the Stork Club. He was wonderful to us during our time in New York. He seemed to have a few favorites in the company, and we were happy to be among them. Joe attended many performances. He invited us out after many of them. Invitations for those occasions always came with a small but expensive gift accompanied by a small envelope inside of which was a small typewritten note extolling our virtues as he saw them. We have kept these as mementos. Joe made us think of an earlier era with stage-door Johnnies.

Here is an example of one of the many notes he sent.

> "Christine dear: - Your lyrical, plastic grace has been evident in every role you have undertaken since the start of this memorable season of ballet. Here is a small tribute to your artistry and charm. May it bring you a small portion of the happiness knowing you has been to your affectionate and very devoted—Joe
>
> Joseph Cameron Cross."

We went to the Sherry Netherland again, when Sol Hurok gave us a dinner party the night before our last performance.

Sol Hurok, or Jolly Solly as we called him, was a well-known impresario, having presented many famous artists and ballet companies over the years. He was thought to be taking a big gamble when he arranged to have the Sadler's Wells Ballet appear in New York with a three-act ballet. But he struck lucky, as the company was such an enormous success not only in New York but across the States and Canada.

Our last night was understandably bittersweet. We didn't want to leave New York; I don't think the audience wanted us to leave. Margot had an ecstatic send-off—screams and shouts. American audiences are very enthusiastic.

5. Tour Including Chicago.

From New York, we took a train to Washington, D.C. Following Danny Kaye's advice, we visited the Lincoln Memorial, the Reflecting Pool and the Washington Memorial with its glorious view of the city.

Performances were to be held in Constitution Hall, not really a theatre. The stage looked and felt as though it had been covered in greasy tar. It was terrifying, with everyone slipping and sliding, including Margot on her entrance in *Lac* Act II. She recovered beautifully. But Moira did not fare so well when she slipped in the "Blue Bird" *pas de deux*. Anyhow, the critics seemed fully aware of the inadequacies of the stage and gave us very good reviews.

We had two shows the next day. And the place was getting on our nerves. It was very hot, the orchestra tuned up right outside our dirty, cramped dressing rooms, and the soles of our pointe shoes were coated in black grease. We all felt better attending an elegant post-show reception at the British Embassy.

The next day we performed at the Mosque in Richmond, Virginia. Then we were off to Philadelphia. Again, during performances at the Academy of Music, we were slipping and sliding. But the audience didn't seem to notice.

The following day, sporting some of our special wardrobe, we girls were taken to a big department store for a publicity shoot. Philadelphia reminded us a bit of Manchester.

Our next stop was Chicago, and we experienced for the first time American sleeping cars—very comfortable, and we slept well. We were supposed to be met in Chicago by members of the Chicago Ballet Society and a pipe band, organized by Ann Barzel, a ballet critic. But because the train was four hours late, we arrived at the Sherman Hotel after a short bus tour of the city. Before we left England, when our friends heard we were going to Chicago, they warned us to look out for the gangsters. So it was rather ironic when we heard later that, just before our arrival at the hotel, a suspicious-looking man had gone up to the reception desk to pay his bill. But the hotel security guards thought that, as he reached for his wallet, he was taking out a gun. They allegedly shot him dead, and the body had been removed shortly before we arrived. Despite the disturbing incident, we enjoyed the hotel (now the State of Illinois building) and its fun restaurant, The Well of the Sea, where we had many good meals after our performances, and the College Inn, where we were entertained by a delightful floor show.

On our first visit to the Civic Opera House, where we were to perform, we were surprised to find it housed in a high-rise building. Nevertheless, it was a joy to be in a real theatre again.

Prior to our opening, Chicago's most influential critic, Claudia Cassidy, had written a nasty anti-British, anti-Sadler's Wells Ballet review. So we were determined to prove her wrong. And we did. *The Sleeping Beauty* was a great success with the audience, and Margot was superb as usual. Cassidy gave us a good review and called Margot a *ballerina assoluta*, which delighted us.

Chicago, nicknamed "The Windy City", was living up to its name. It was a bitterly cold wind, too, not conducive to sightseeing. But we walked to State Street and admired the Christmas decorations. We stayed in Chicago from December 13 to 20. On our last night, Margot did the most fantastic "Rose Adagio." She held one attitude so long, afterwards Robert Irving—who was conducting—said that, next time it happens, he would go out for coffee.

We continued on to Lansing, Michigan, home to one of the most famous agricultural colleges in America. We performed in the college auditorium. We had hoped the audience might appreciate the "Milking" scene in *Façade*. But they were unresponsive, and even Margot's *Lac* did nothing to enthuse them. We got strange but good notices.

Our next stop was Toronto, Canada, at the Royal Alexandra. The cold and snow followed us. Although the theatre was old and small, the audiences were so appreciative— yet without the continual interruptions of applause from American audiences.

A member of my family, Hubert Du Boulay, turned up. He was a dear, reminding me of Grandpa. He and his wife took us out to lunch and showed us some family photos.

While in Toronto, we were driven to see Niagara Falls. It was a dull and bitterly cold day, but not snowing. The spray from the Falls had frozen over everything nearby, an extraordinary effect. We were shown down to the tunnel underneath the Falls, and had to don huge "macs" and boots for the walk along the tunnel, where we could see water rushing over us, only about three feet away.

From city to city, we were entertained by many kind people, some even helping us with our luggage and driving us to the train station. We arrived in Ottawa at noon and were invited to tea at the Government House by Lord Alexander. He and his wife showed us some of the lovely rooms. We left at night. I remember the snow was deep, and the houses and lights gave everything a fairytale look—like a Christmas card.

After a good performance at the Capital, we attended a formal event at the High Commissioner of Canada's House. As he was ill, his wife, Lady Clutterbuck, was hosting for him. Back on the train, our "hotel", we couldn't sleep. So we found a place to party, as someone had a bottle of liquor. Then Bobby joined us—a little drunk, he entertained us with amusing stories.

After arriving in Montreal, we went to the hotel and slept well. After lunch, we walked to the theatre, His Majesty's, about ten minutes away. But it was still so cold. We were frozen when we got to the tiny and dirty theatre. The performance went well, except for a terrible commotion during the *Lac* Act II waltz. It eventually quieted down, and the waltz got a terrific reception. Evidently, there had been a small fire somewhere in the front. The audience in the stalls started to panic.

Despite the snow and the bitter cold, we managed to do quite a lot of Christmas shopping. We got some presents to bring home or send by parcel. Everything was so tempting. We worried about the weight of our luggage, which was bulging. Customs men came to the theatre to check our theatre baskets. They found something in one, and so made a search of each and every one. Fortunately, ours were alright. So we went out and celebrated, and had enormous steaks—our last dinner before flying home.

Our fears about overweight luggage were unfounded. All was well. All our dollars had been spent, so we borrowed a few to have a little lunch before boarding the plane. We hated leaving in many ways, but were cheered by de Valois saying we would be returning.

6. Back In London. George Balanchine.

We left Montreal on December 21st, so we were back home in time for Christmas. But we opened again at the Opera House on Boxing Day, December 26th, performing *Cinderella*.

When the curtain rose, with Margot, Bobby and Fred alone on the stage, we were sure they would receive an ovation after all the glory they brought the company on the American tour. But they were met with silence. We were all so upset; maybe we had become too used to the enthusiasm of the American audience and forgotten how reserved the English were. But it was good to be back in our beloved Opera House.

The year saw the premiere of de Valois' new ballet, *Don Quixote*, which was not one of our favorites. The music was difficult, and Madam had trouble getting us to count it correctly. At one rehearsal, she asked a group of us what count we had reached. We answered 49, or some such improbable number. She was not happy with us, and we were not happy either.

In April 1950, George Balanchine came from New York to stage his *Ballet Imperial* for the company. Rehearsals were intense over a three-week period. But he was impressed with how quickly we learned it. Most of us enjoyed the ballet and working with Balanchine.

In retrospect, I often think of how lucky we were to have had such a direct link with the great Diaghilev. Our connection with Ninette de Valois, Alicia Markova, Ursula Moreton, Alexandra Danilova, Stanislas Idzikowski, Anton Dolin, George Balanchine and Léonide Massine, all of whom worked for Diaghilev.

7. Return To The Villa.

In the summer of 1950, we returned to Beaulieu. We called our rental car MABEL after the last name initials of the five of us who went to France this tim: Lorna Mossford, Brian Ashbridge, Christine du Boulay, Richard Ellis and Rosemary Lindsay. As before, David was at the villa, but Michael was not. And, as before, we went there almost every day. Gillian Lynne (now of *Cats* fame) spent time with us, too. Julia Farron and her new husband, Alfred Rodrigues, also joined us one day. On that day, there was a brief thunderstorm just as we were about to have lunch on the harbor wall. So we hurried inside the villa, with David leading the way—right down into the dungeon, which we had never seen before. The dungeon was huge, with a prison cell, statues of men on horseback and men in armor, and a long wooden refectory table with chairs. So we sat at the table and ate our lunch, purposefully spilling a little wine (blood) while the thunder and lightning enhanced the dramatic setting.

Years later, Richard and I returned to Cap Ferrat. We were spending a night in Nice, hoping to look at the villa again. We walked in vain, seeing no high building. But we did find a gate that looked familiar. We entered and saw a low building, yet the Italianate entrance was still visible. A French servant, upon hearing of our association with the old building, told us that the new American owners had made all the changes. It was sad. They say never go back.

Chapter V
Second American Tour: 1950-1951

1. New York.

On our return from France, we spent the month of August at Covent Garden for the whole of August preparing for our second, more extensive tour of the States. Once more, the girls were given complete outfits and, this time, the boys were given some clothes. We left on September 5th. I wrote a daily diary, which I sent weekly from the States to my mother. On our return, she gave it back to me, and I used it as my reference to our U.S. visit.

Our plane to New York was a Flying Fortress, with the bomb bay converted into a bar, which we used on our flight to Iceland. After an hour there, we continued to New York, arriving ahead of schedule, thus thwarting the press

Richard and I stayed in a hotel with the company this time because Fred Franklin was in town. We saw him at his apartment on our first evening. Happily, he was only going on a short tour with the Ballet Russe and would be back in town for most of our visit. We saw Joe Cross again, and he took Freddie and us to the Ritz-Carlton for dinner and then to the Drake.

The season opened on September 10th in 90-degree heat with *Le Lac des Cygnes* to a wonderful reception—though not quite as ecstatic as our very first. Margot danced beautifully as always. Afterwards, Joe took a few of us to Longchamps and brought along the always charming and amusing Alexandra Danilova.

So many people asked us out, it seemed that almost every night we were invited to a house or treated to dinner mostly by dancers and New York ballet teachers.

On one of our days off, Gillian Lynne, Gerd Larsen, Ray Powell and Richard and I decided to go to Long Island. We found a lovely spot called Glen Cove, which reminded us of the Isle of Wight, with its small bay and moored boats. The sun shone all day. Gillian and Ray went for a swim, but it wasn't warm enough for the rest of us. Then we went in search of food and drink. We found what looked like a deserted yacht club, with only a little man in charge. He said there was no food, but we could have drinks. He had no idea how to mix them and told us to mix our own. So Richard got behind the bar and took over. Great fun. To finish the good day, we found an Italian restaurant and had a marvelous meal. We got the train back just in time to get ready for a cocktail party at the Sherry Netherland Hotel, given by a good friend of Fred's, Alice Bouverie. She had been an Astor, an Oblensky and a Hoffmanstahl—and apparently owned a lot of New York.

One evening, Joe took us to dinner with friends of his, the Borgias (we loved the name). They lived in a lovely old brownstone house, where we sat on the floor by a big fireplace and enjoyed a delicious Italian meal with Chianti (no poison).

Fred invited us to see a rehearsal of the Ballet Russe, which we thoroughly enjoyed. That evening we saw an excellent show at the Copacabana. Joe E. Lewis was the headliner.

The day before our last performance in New York, Joe Cross invited us to his place for lunch. There were about eight of us. We had banded together and bought him a present of a silver-and-crystal cocktail shaker, as he had been so very kind to us. He seemed delighted.

We finished the season with two *Sleeping Beauty*'s. Moira did the matinée. She was dancing so well as Aurora. After the matinée, we went to Fred's to say a sad farewell to him and a couple of his close friends. We all had such a wonderful time together this year.

2. On Tour.

On October 2ⁿᵈ, we were bussed to Penn Station and boarded a train to Philadelphia, where it was very hot. We performed at the Royal Academy of Music, with a small raked stage, which felt so strange after the Met. A Mr. Strawbridge, a Philadelphia entrepreneur, entertained the company with cocktails, dinner and dancing.

The management informed us that we could take only one piece of luggage each for the rest of the tour until we got to Los Angeles. Richard and I were very pleased with ourselves as we got all we needed into one case.

After New York, we found the Philly audiences disappointing. They hardly laughed during *Façade*. *Giselle* went a little better. I think they were more concerned about the baseball World Series between the Yankees and the Phillies. Richard and I were out walking one day, when we were stopped by a stranger who asked, "What's the score?" They had asked the wrong people. We had no idea what they were talking about. We later realized it was World Series time.

We returned to our special train after the last performance. There were six sleeping cars, plus a dining car. Earlier Bertie Hughes, our manager, had asked Richard as Equity representative to help him allocate the cars to the company. Richard suggested the orchestra be in one and the partying ones in another, and so on. The good thing about having our own cars meant we could get up in the morning and go to the dining car for breakfast in our robes.

We arrived in Pittsburg on October 6ᵗʰ. The stage of the Syrian Mosque, where we performed, was slippery. But somehow Margot and Moira danced beautifully.

Then we were off to Atlanta. During the train ride, Richard and I started what was to be our chief diversion on our long journeys—playing Canasta, usually with Robert Irving and Ray Powell and Pamela May.

We arrived in Atlanta, to lovely weather, on October 9ᵗʰ. A well-known family invited most of us to their home for a Southern breakfast. We were driven there by a caravan of cars. Our driver knew lots of London theatre people, including Denis.

The plantation house was a typical Southern mansion. After dining on the wide lawn, we went to see the cotton fileds—the ones used in the film, *Gone with the Wind*. Our driver then took us on a tour of Atlanta. He was most interesting and told us about Margaret Mitchell, the author of *Gone with the Wind*, who was a great friend of our hosts. He took us to the famous Cylclorama depicting the Civil War. We drank our first mint juleps and tasted sugar cane. Another first in Atlanta was going to a Bar-B-Q drive-in, where they brought our food on trays and attached them to the car window ledge.

Unfortunately, during this time, many people were off—including my only doubles in two ballets—leaving me in every ballet and every act for a while.

Birmingham, Alabama was next: another large barn of a theatre, the Municipal Auditorium.

Then we were off to New Orleans. We were looking forward to it so much, and then the train was three hours late—infuriating as we only had a day and a half there. It was very hot, so we had to buy cooler clothes. We finally got to the hotel, unpacked, cleaned up, had a bite to eat and went out on the town. It was warm, sunny. We went to Canal Street, the French Quarter and Bourbon Street.

In the evening, the performance seemed to be a success—even in another huge auditorium.

Afterwards, we hoped to go to the famous restaurant, Antoines but it was closed. So we went to Pat O'Briens with Ray, Henry Legerton, Gillian and Gerd, then to the Court of Two Sisters, where we sat and ate under banana trees. We returned to Bourbon Street, which at night was dazzling, with all the lights and night clubs. But there were some dives, too. At one, the stripper was pregnant. After a visit to the Old Absinthe Bar, we finally returned to the hotel at 4:00 a.m. Following our second performance, we were back on the train and off to Houston.

Our hotel there was the famous Shamrock Hotel, with its shamrock-shaped pool, which we all rushed to as soon as we could, so lovely and refreshing. We were sure the Texans were a little alarmed when hordes of young things invaded the pool.

The Houston theatre was also the Municipal Auditorium. After our second performance, it was back to our "hotel" and off on the long trip to Los Angeles—a three-day, two-night journey. I remember hoping to see a lone cowboy riding through the tall cactus. My wish came true when I woke up one morning and looked out of the train window and saw just that.

We made short stops at Yuma and El Paso, where the temperature was 110 degrees when we strolled on the platform. But it was exciting to be riding along the Rio Grande and be so near to Mexico.

During the three-day train ride to Los Angeles, we had a party one night in our car. Bobby joined us and brought a bottle of liquor. It was a fun time—even when de Valois walked through, and we became concerned. But all she said was that it smelled like a four-ale bar and left.

3. Los Angeles and San Francisco.

We arrived in Los Angeles on October 18th. We took a cab to the Ambassador Hotel, passing so many places we had heard about or seen on the movie screen.

Oscar Berlin, the man from the Hurok office who was in charge of our transport and luggage, had become a good friend. He came to our room soon after our arrival to say that he had rented a car for a few days. We started with a drive down Wilshire Boulevard, about ten miles all the way to the coast. At last we saw the Pacific Ocean, and on a beautiful moonlit night.

To get to the theatre, we had to rely on chartered buses: a bit restricting. This is a fabulous town, even though everything is so spread out and far apart.

We opened on October 19th at the Shrine Auditorium with *The Sleeping Beauty*. Margot was wonderful, and the audience was enthusiastic. Many Hollywood stars were in the audience, and we heard their names being announced after the show as their cars came for them: Mr. and Mrs. Clark Gable, the Oliviers, Ida Lupino, Joseph Cotton, Greer Garson.

Sol Hurok gave a party. Again there were many celebrities—Greer Garson, Joseph Cotton, Charlie Chaplin, Tony Martin, Barry Fitzgerald and Gene Tierney.

The day before, while we were driving down Wilshire Boulevard, a car drove up beside us with Gene Tierney at the wheel. She looked as beautiful as she did at the party. We also drove to the Hollywood Bowl and saw Grauman's Theatre, where the stars leave their hand and foot prints in the concrete outside.

One day we were able to drive to the coast again, passing Malibu Beach and on to Zuma Beach—a long beach with the hills coming right down to the coastal road.

During our second week in Los Angeles, we were taken in groups to various movie studios. We were in a group going to Warner Bros. On our arrival there, we were escorted to the dining room, where we were introduced to some of the stars who would be showing us around: Doris Day, Ruth Roman, Patricia Neal, Phyllis Thaxter, Gene Nelson and Steve Cochran. We missed seeing Vivien Leigh because she was on location with *A Streetcar Named Desire*, and John Wayne was not there, which disappointed Richard. At one studio, we saw Joan Crawford and Robert Young on a set. She was having a difficult scene. I'm afraid our presence didn't help, and the director asked us to leave.

October 28th was our last day in Los Angeles. Richard hurt his back again, but not too badly.

We boarded an ordinary passenger train to San Francisco. It was dark and raining when we arrived, and Richard went straight to bed to rest his back.

The Opera House, near the hotel, had nice dressing rooms, but we did not like the stage. We didn't like the first-night audience either. Moira's Aurora was lovely, but even she did not wake up the audience.

Ninette was rehearsing us so much in order that *Rake's Progress*, *Les Patineurs* and *Façade* would have double casts to help distribute the work more evenly.

Richard was having daily back treatment and otherwise lying in bed.

Oscar got another car. Nadia Nerina, Alexander Grant and I went with him for a drive across the Golden Gate Bridge and on to the Muir Woods. The view on the way home was breathtaking—the gorgeous autumn coloring, the bay and the skyline. We went to Fisherman's Wharf and Telegraph Hill. We came down Russian Hill, so windy and steep, one is not allowed up it. Back at the hotel, I found a note from Richard. The doctor had said he was better and could go out for a while. So he had gone out with John (Jack) Hart and Margaret Dale. Later, Richard felt better. The two of us went and had a lobster dinner at Fisherman's Warf. We took a bus to Nob's Hill, where we sat at the "Top of the Mark" in the Mark Hopkins Hotel and watched a beautiful sunset from a window table. We decided that, so far, this was the most livable city in America.

4. More Tour. Half-way Party.

Once again we had to pack into one case for more one-night stands. The last night was very good; maybe the audience had been too stunned to clap. But we were sad to leave San Francisco. The weather had broken and we left in the rain for Sacramento, where we gave two performances.

Denver was the next—our half-way stop. So we thought it would be fun to throw a costume party. We were in Browns Hotel and arranged for a party room. We limited everyone to a small amount of money. Richard decided to go as "Scarface", and I as a bottle of Schaparelli "Shocking". I bought rolls of amber-colored cellophane paper and Scotch tape, flowers for around my "bottle" neck, paper doilies and gold paper for the base and wide ribbon. All Richard needed was make-up for his scar, a ghastly tie and his suit.

November 17th was the day of the party.

The performance went very well, but some of us found it exhausting dancing in the mile-high atmosphere. The theatre provided oxygen machines for us. Margot and others used them during *Lac*.

After the performance, we rushed back to the hotel to dress and prepare for our party.

I had fun getting into my costume—sticking all the cellophane and making the ribbon to look like the measuring tape with Schaparelli "Shocking" written on it.

It was one of the best parties. Such ingenuity—some of the creations were marvelous and all made with so little. Fred Ashton was the chief judge. I got first prize for the most beautiful costume, and Pauline Clayden for the most original. She had covered herself from head to toe in bandages, with a card on her chest saying "The Prospect Before Us" (also the name of a de Valois ballet).

Friends of Julia Farron took us for a drive up into the snow-capped mountains. We also visited Central City, a gold-rush ghost town that looked like a movie set. On the way back to Denver, we passed the tracks of old stage coaches and abandoned gold mines.

On to Lincoln, Nebraska, where it was cold and snowing. We danced in the University Auditorium on a slippery stage that was really a basketball court. There were no dressing rooms, so we had to change in the swimming pool lockers without any seats or mirrors.

We arrived in Des Moines, Iowa early the next morning; we did one show and returned to the train to Omaha. For the first time, we had an almost empty house for the matinée. Apparently, they had only advertised the evening performance. But Margot was dancing better than ever, despite all the traveling. Why did we complain?

On Thanksgiving Day, we were off to Tulsa, changing trains in Kansas City. Moira was feeling lonely, so we took her with us to see *King Solomon's Mines*. Then we enjoyed a delicious Thanksgiving dinner back at the hotel.

We heard the weather was bad over much of the States—torrential rain in California; a blizzard in Cleveland; and bitter cold in Tulsa. The stage in Tulsa was small and dirty. There were no mirrors in the dressing rooms, no cross-over and one toilet—the only place with water, which we had to share with the audience.

We were glad to leave and go to Dallas. The stage there was the Starlight State Fair Auditorium. Dallas was also home to the famous Neiman-Marcus store, where the Christmas decorations were beautiful.

In Dallas and in much of the South, we witnessed racial segregation, especially on the buses. In Atlanta, New Orleans and Texas, there were separate quarters for blacks and whites—in the theatres and on public transporation. Inside the buses, there were boards saying Whites on them, which were moved according to the number of white passengers. I was on a bus full of white passengers. A black youngster got on and had to ask a white youngster to move so that he could sit in the right section—otherwise he would have been fined.

We got to Oklahoma City on November 28th. Margot did one of her best "Rose Adagio's" in another vast auditorium. But the audience was so far away, we seemed to have no contact with them.

Since we had no hotel, we found it cheaper and warmer to go to see a film. In the last two cities we had seen films with Doris Day, Ruth Roman and Steve Cochran in them. It was fun to see them, having just met them in person.

Memphis was our next stop, another big stage but wonderful audience. Everywhere we go now, we are so impressed with the Christmas decorations.

We all decided to leave immediately after the show and go to St. Louis, where we could stay in a hotel on our day off there.

The Henry Kiel Auditorium in St. Louis is really two in one. The ballet was in one; the circus was in the other. We spent ages watching exciting circus acts. I felt like a six-year-old again experiencing my first circus.

Our first performance was a matinée, and we arrived in pouring rain. There was a terrific thunderstorm. We had never seen or heard anything like it. Our English storms are mild compared to this. So far , St. Louis had looked to us like Manchester.

Whenever we could, we watched the circus in awe of some of the incredible acts and we met some of the performers, who were so nice. We asked them to come and see us, so they came though the pass door and stood in the wings. Our admiration was mutual I think.

To get to Bloomington, Indiana, our next stop, we were on an uncomfortable ordinary train. It made a stop in the middle of nowhere because it had a "hot-box"—whatever that was. We all got out and "invaded" a small café nearby. Two of the boys acted as waiters, as there were so many of us.

Bloomington is a small university town with a very nice auditorium. We gave one performance there, and then on to Lafayette, where the train arrived in the middle of the street. Strange to us.

Our next stop was Detroit. We were performing in the Municipal Auditorium, which was quite a walk from our hotel. It was still damp and cold. We had matinées and evening performances, not leaving us much time to look around. But after the first evening performance, we did go to a Burlesque Theatre—our first—which was entertaining.

December 11th. On the train to Cleveland, we passed a frozen Lake Erie.

The hotel was across the street from the theatre, the Public Auditorium, and 7,500 people were in the audience for *The Sleeping Beauty*.

From Cleveland we went to Cincinnati, where all I remember is losing $100—all the money I had saved up to buy family Christmas presents. But we were looking forward to our next stop, Chicago, where we could settle down for more than two days.

5. Chicago. Christmas.

We arrived in Chicago on December 17th and stayed at the Sherman House.

On our first night, we were all invited to a reception at the University of Chicago, quite a drive away. All we got were coffee and sandwiches, but we met some very nice people.

A group of us had been planning a special party as we were going to be in Chicago for Christmas. So we had a meeting to discuss further plans. I also went to a dime store and bought some decorations for our room.

The first night was a very social one. After the performance, Ruth Page invited us all to a black-tie party at the Racquet Club. We were plied with champagne on our arrival. Ruth was a Chicago dance celebrity and had been in the Diaghilev Ballet. She took the company to a separate room, where we were seated and given a huge meal. She knew how to treat dancers.

Quite a few of the *South Pacific* cast members were there, too. A young Cuban girl, who played Bloody Mary, sang and danced for us, and then asked for a partner. Ray volunteered. He was great.

Margot looked stunning in a Dior dress, a sea-green sheath covered in pearly sequins. She looked like a mermaid. The dress had a little panel at the back, like a train, which she removed when she got up to dance to reveal a little slit in the back. About eight of us were the last to leave around 3:30 a.m.

The next day, Claudia Cassidy gave us a very good review and said how delicious Margot was at the party. Cassidy sat next to her at dinner.

December 21st. Since we were going to be spending Christmas in Chicago, David Webster (the Administrator of Covent Garden Opera House) arranged for us to have a Christmas party in the hotel and provided most of the food. But three of us, all wives, decided we wanted to do something special on our own. We would prepare an English trifle. So off we went to buy the ingredients. I asked the hotel manager if he could provide a large bowl for the trifle and if he could find a Santa Claus costume—which he did. I also came away with a bottle of bourbon.

December 23rd. We performed two *Lacs,* which didn't leave much time for preparations. Our committee—which was made up of Gillian, Pauline Clayden, Bryan, Fred Ashton, Richard and I—decided on the food and drinks. Rod (Alfred Rodrigues) was arranging a cabaret with company members, and Alex was going to show the film he had taken of us on tour.

Christmas Eve. It was hard to concentrate during two *Sleeping Beauty's.* Our minds were on other things—mainly the party, and our visions of how dress up the ballet. We longed to decorate the palace columns with strands of holly; to have a Mistletoe Fairy; and wrap all the fairy's gifts as Christmas presents. Carabosse would appear as Santa Claus. It would have been fun.

After the evening performance, we rushed back to the hotel to finish making the trifle, except for the cream. All of this was done in our bathroom on a tiny electric ring and saucepan. We then gave it to the kitchen staff to keep for us until the big day. During this time, company members kept coming to our room with their presents for other dancers. Because Richard and I had the biggest room, we were the keepers of all the presents. Our closet was full.

Christmas Day. We awoke to a white Christmas. Four of us had been invited to lunch with the Assistant British Consul. There we met a man who knew some Du Boulay's and who came from Ballina, County Mayo. He knew the Knox's and Templeogue, near Sally Park.

We then went to the Consul's home and found Margot and a friend, Moira with her fiancé Ludovic Kennedy, Bob Irving, Leslie and Ray. We couldn't stay long because we had to get back to organize the party room.

The hotel had provided a tree, which helped a lot to make the room more festive. Richard and I brought down all the presents (about 80) and arranged them around the tree. Meanwhile, poor Pauline was having an awful time getting the cream for the trifle to thicken. It was too warm. After much beating, the trifle was ready. It was a big success—naturally, since we used half a bottle of sherry in it.

The cabaret, which followed dinner, was brilliantly organized by Rod. The cast included Julia, Ray, Leslie, Kenneth MacMillan, Gillian, Anne Negus, Valerie Taylor and Rod.

The first number was "Covent Garden Here We Come" to the tune "California", then a preview of *Daphnis and Chloë* to the song "Chloë". Three boys did "We're the Swans They Left Behind in Kansas City" to "Everything's Up To Date In Kansas City". Then "Give our Regards to Madam" to the music of "Give My Regards to Broadway".

Rod's idea of television ads followed this, starting with "Don's Dainty Donuts" to *Don Quixote* music, then "Use Façade the Girdle that Girdles the Earth" to the *Façade* waltz, and finishing up with a goof to "Jingle Bells".

Meanwhile, Bob Irving was changing into his Santa Claus suit. He was announced by Margot, who gave one of her deafening two-finger whistles. Bob was terrific despite being so hot inside his suit and his pants falling down half-way through distributing the gifts. It was a wonderful party, and made up a little for not being home for Christmas.

As I mentioned, we had been unable to see *South Pacific* in New York. But with help from our friend in the company in Chicago, we were able to finally see it. Ray was with us, and we sat and pinched each other. It was even better than we had imagined.

After one performance, the parents of a super in *Lac*, invited about eight of us to their house. It was nice to be in a home again, not the eternal hotel room, and they were very kind.

A few days after Christmas, Julia, Rod, Richard and I went to the studio of the well-known photographer, Maurice Seymour, who had offered us sittings at very low prices. He had photographed so many famous dancers. He did shots of Julia and Richard in *Les Patineurs pas de deux* together and alone; of me in *Dante Sonata*; and head shots of all of us.

December 29th. It was still very cold and snowy, not exactly walking weather. But we did spend time in the famous Marshall Fields, where we bought warm clothes in preparation for Winnipeg. We had been warned that visitors might suffer from frostbite.

We celebrated New Year's Eve in our hotel room with a few close company friends. It was our last night in Chicago. We wished we could stay longer.

6. More Tour.

We left Chicago on New Year's Day and took a train to Winnipeg, passing by the frozen Mississippi.

Paddy Stone, an ex-member of the company, met us in Winnipeg—his home town. He and many of the natives were hatless, while we were all muffled up. Paddy and his family entertained us, as did an English girl and her parents. We finished up a hearty meal with a real pot of tea with boiling water—bliss!

We left Winnipeg on January 5th with the thermometer reading -30 degrees.

The ride to Boston was a long one in a rickety old train, with some of our luggage exposed to the snow and cold. At one point, the lights went out and we had no heat for a while. We happily changed trains in Chicago and were able to play Canasta again.

Once in a snow-covered Boston, we liked the Georgian houses and winding streets.

At our hotel, the water had gone cold just when we were longing for a good hot bath after our endless journey. It had taken 56 hours altogether.

The first-night audience at the Opera House was very appreciative. A party followed at the British Embassy—an abundance of good food and drinks, white ties and medal ribbons. Apparently it was a special night. One dear old man said it was the first time he had been able to wear his C.B.E. Sir Oliver and Lady Franks were there (he was the British Ambassador to the United States). They seemed to be at all our galas. We met the Vice-Consul, the only female one in America. She was thrilled to have us in town, saying it made her job so much easier.

We did our last *Sleeping Beauty* in Boston since it had to be returned to London and refurbished for our opening there.

On January 11th, we were driven to Harvard. We lunched at Harvard University in the huge dining room with about 400 boys and sat with one of the house masters. The next day we did some shopping in a well-known store called Filenes, which had a wonderful bargain basement.

On January 13th, we finished with two *Lac*'s. But during the third act, a little girl who was a page, standing rigidly beside the throne, fainted. The poor child fell flat and broke a tooth and cut her nose. Rod and Richard quickly carried her offstage; she was bleeding profusely. Later all was well, but I doubt she will ever forget her performance with the Sadler's Wells Ballet.

We took a train to New York on our day off, left our luggage at the station and then went to the Wellington Hotel. The next day we were driven in two buses to White Plains and to the Westchester County Center, a barn of a place, and the audience was dreary. Then we were taken back to a train that didn't leave until two o'clock in the morning. While in New York, we noticed quite a few bomb-shelter signs and heard talk of an atom bomb. One of the newspapers had published a cartoon of Manhattan after an atom-bomb attack. It was a horrible thought. Before leaving, we met friends at the Russian Tea Room to say our farewells.

Next stop: Toronto. When we arrived, we were told our rooms weren't ready. But as on a few occasions before, Richard worked some magic, and we got ours quickly.

It was nearing the end of the tour, and we grew tired of going to receptions. I'm afraid we were starting to behave badly, sitting in a group together rather than having to make small talk.

But Richard and I did see Hubert Du Boulay and his wife again, and one performance made it all worthwhile. Margot danced a wonderful Swan Queen, and the audience stamped and shouted.

On January 20th, we were off to Ottawa and Government House for cocktails. Different members of the staff took groups of us to their homes for dinner.

The snow had turned to freezing rain—an effect that made everything look like crystal. But the roads were a solid sheet of ice. We were driven safely back to our hotel.

Again, Margot performed a beautiful *Lac,* and the audience went wild. But after the *Mazurka* which Richard and I were in, dancing one of the two lead couples, we got two calls—much to the annoyance of the *Czardas*. Margot jokingly hissed at us from the wings.

On January 23rd, after a two-and-a-half-hour journey to Montreal, we found ourselves in the filthy St. Denis Theatre. Down the middle of the dressing room we all shared was a trough of water. It was located in the basement, with only partitions between the boys', girls', wardrobe and orchestra—most unpleasant. I was on in every ballet. The only nice thing was meeting another family member, Philip Du Boulay.

Leaving some luggage at the BOAC office, we were off to Quebec. We were told that the train station in Montreal was near the hotel. So we and a few others decided to walk there but soon realized we were going to the wrong station. We squeezed into a taxi and flew off to the right station, only to find our train had just left. The station master told us not to worry and recommended we take a taxi to the next station, which would take about ten minutes. The train would take 20 minutes. All's well that ends well. We got there before the train and boarded it much to the relief of the rest of the company.

In Quebec, we stayed at the Chateau Fontenac. The snow was quite deep, and it felt even colder than Winnipeg.

It was our last and 43rd *Lac* performed to a strangely unenthusiastic audience.

Time to return home to London. There were some romances on the tour. Some dancers were going home with heavy hearts, and a few were planning to return and get married.

Hurok gave us a wonderful party at the Chateau Fontenac. But as we had so many times on this tour, we felt guilty eating so much good food thinking of the lack of it at home.

On January 30th, after some delays, we finally took off for our flight from Montreal to London. It amazed us how the plane ever took off. There were many more of us on this one flight, plus much more luggage. The captain announced on our arrival that, in all his 21 years of flying, he had never made the trip so fast. We had taken fifteen minutes off the scheduled time. After all our worries about the customs, we need not have. The customs men didn't open a thing—we could have brought in the Crown Jewels.

We let out a big whoop of joy when we touched down. Home again! But we wouldn't have missed this tour for anything.

7. Back To London. Richard Leaves The Company.

On returning to England, Richard seriously thought about what to do next. His back was still a problem. We received an offer to start a ballet school in Chicago, which was very tempting. We both liked America so much on both the tours.

Then during a rehearsal of *Daphnis and Chloë*, the new ballet by Frederick Ashton, Richard hurt his back again. It was the final straw.

He went to see Madam, and explained the whole situation. She was so understanding, saying that since he was an "old boy," he could continue to receive his salary for the next six months. He also could have access to all aspects of stage management and watch any classes at the school to study the teaching methods. This was such a generous offer, and Richard made the most of it. He became assistant stage manager for the revival of *The Fairy Queen* at the Royal Opera House and spent many days at the Ballet School observing classes.

The offer to teach in Chicago had come from a woman we had met on our second visit there. She had approached Ray Powell. He declined because he wanted to stay on with the company. Knowing our situation, he suggested we take the offer. Thus started long and serious correspondence on the possibility of going to America.

We finally agreed that Richard would go to Chicago first, starting in January 1952, to see how things worked out.

During his 13 years with the Sadler's Wells Ballet—excluding the five-and-a-half years in the Royal Navy—Richard performed in 43 ballets, 17 of which he was in the premiere performance and five of them in roles created for him. He partnered Margot Fonteyn, Pearl Argyle, Moira Shearer, Violetta Elvin, Beryl Grey, Pamela May and Julia Farron, to name a few. His teachers included Stanislas Idzikowski, Margaret Craske, Ninette de Valois, Ursula Moreton and Vera Volkova.

I continued in the company. One of the great joys was working on Ashton's *Daphnis and Chloë*. Everyone involved felt it was something special. We were all so disappointed by the cool reception it received on the first night. We couldn't understand the audience or the critics. It took a while before both came around to seeing the ballet for the gem it was.

Massine came again to create a new work, *Donald of the Burthens*, based on a Scottish theme. We were not too enthused about Massine and his funny steps being applied to Scottish steps.

Ashton also created another new ballet, *Tiresius*, with music by Constant Lambert, who died tragically a few weeks after the first performance.

In one section, the *corps* moved slowly in a long procession. At that time, there were quite a few minor injuries among the dancers, most of whom were being treated at St. Bartholomew's Hospital. That particular section of *Tiresius* was ideal for them, and many appeared in what became known as the "Bart's Brigade".

I have often been asked which were my favorite ballets to be in. A hard question. It is almost easier to say which ones I didn't like, which were few. Oft times, one's pleasure dancing in a ballet is due to one's emotional or physical well being or audience reaction.

I loved the classics for their diversity, the mixture of *corps* work and character dances. I think *Coppélia* was my favorite, especially when I danced in the International Ballet and was one of Swanilda's friends and Prayer, and later in the Sadler's Wells Ballet, dancing the lead *Mazurka* couple with Richard.

The Rake's Progress and *Hamlet* were favorites, too, because I loved dramatic ballets. *Giselle* was another favorite—the drama, the music and because it was the first ballet I had danced in professionally. During my professional career, I performed in 37 ballets, ten of which I was in the original cast.

Chapter VI
America: 1952-1959

1. Richard To Chicago. Allegro School of Ballet.

On January 9th, 1952, the evening before Richard was to leave for America, a group of his close friends arranged a party for him in our flat. It was a difficult time for him thinking about going off alone to the unknown so far away. We thought we would drown his nervousness in a good stiff drink. So we prepared a martini to the top of a cocktail shaker. He didn't feel much after that.

The next morning, I took Richard to the station and saw him off to Liverpool. On the train journey there, he said he shed a few tears. I shed a few tears, too. I was nervous for Richard and already lonely.

At Liverpool he boarded the *Franconia*, a passenger liner that had transported troops during the war. He was in a room mid-ship on the lower deck with three other men. Half-way across the Atlantic, they struck a bad storm, and the boat literally did not move. Richard felt it was about to break in two right where he was.

Eventually they reached New York, and Richard went to the apartment of one of the Ballet Russe de Monte Carlo dancers, who offered to put Richard up for the night since Freddie was out of town.

The next day he took the train to Chicago, where he was met by Mrs. C. and a friend of hers called Jean. Richard was to live with Mrs. C. and her husband in the Hyde Park area. It was a nice apartment, In fact Mr. and Mrs. C. and their daughter had entertained some of us on our last tour.

The first order of things was to find a location for the proposed ballet school. Space was found in the downtown Kimball Building at Wabash and Jackson, just by the el tracks. Richard and Mr. C. started work on transforming it into a ballet studio, arranging dressing rooms and office space, and putting up barres and a mirror.

Richard immediately started teaching a few very small classes in temporary locations. Soon, though, the Allegro School of Ballet officially opened. One of his first students was a very talented teenager named Dido Sayers, who later would join the New York City Ballet. Her father Lionel, the timpanist and chief librarian of the Chicago Symphony Orchestra, would become a good friend.

A few days after Richard's arrival, Ruth Page and her husband Tom Fisher invited him to dinner. Richard delivered a letter to Ruth from Margot Fonteyn. Thanks to Larry Long, Ruth's ballet master who, going through some of Ruth's belongings after her death, found the letter and returned it to Richard. In the letter, Margot explained that Richard had just left the company to start teaching in Chicago, and would Ruth please cheer him up since he was terrified. She added that he couldn't feel as bad as the pioneers in covered wagons. She said that I would be following him. Tom and Ruth were friendly to Richard, but they quizzed him mercilessly on the whys and wherefores of his coming to Chicago.

Meanwhile, in London, Rosemary Lindsay came to stay with me at Devonshire Terrace. We had been good friends since our student days at the Sadler's Wells Ballet School. It was nice to have a companion during Richard's absence. He was wonderful about writing to me. I had many lovely, long typewritten letters (he always preferred typing) I, of course, wrote often to him. One time he received a sweet note from Margot saying that "Dream-Girl" was looking sad and missing him.

The month after Richard left for America, King George VI died and we had a new monarch, Elizabeth II. The King's funeral procession passed near Lancaster Gate, so I went and stood with the crowds along the way. I saw the young Queen and Prince Philip in her coach and the King's brothers, including Edward, Duke of Windsor, walking behind the hearse.

Just before I left for Chicago, Fred Ashton gave a farewell party for me in his beautiful London home. It was a bittersweet occasion as was leaving the company. Nearly all my dear friends were company members I knew I would miss, but I was longing to be with Richard again and join him in our new life. We would still be part of the ballet world, which neither of us wished to leave.

2. Christine To Chicago.

As classes at the Allegro school progressed, matters between Mrs. C. and Richard did not. In his weekly letters, Richard explained his frustrations over her behavior. He finally told her he thought it would help if I came over, too. She said she couldn't afford another teacher, but agreed in the end. So early in April 1952, I said goodbye to friends and relatives and my native land. My father came to Southampton to see me off on the Queen Mary. He had some connection with the captain—a nice perk since, the next day, I was invited with a few others to cocktails in his cabin. It was a pleasant voyage—a far cry from Richard's uncomfortable, rough and lonely crossing. I arrived in New York on April 15th and was met by Freddie Franklin, who took me to a friend's apartment where I was to spend the night. That evening, we all met at Joe Cross' place and, as always, he treated me royally.

The next day they they saw me to the train to Chicago, where I had a wonderful reunion with Richard. He booked a hotel room for us for that night.

We talked at length about the unpleasant school situation and how it was quite impossible for him to reason with Mrs. C. I said surely it couldn't be that bad. But after a week, I realized it was. Nevertheless, we had no choice except to cope as best we could. After all, she was our sponsor (for which we will always be grateful) and, because she was paying us so little, we couldn't afford to go anywhere else.

A little help came a short time after I arrived. Lucille Stoddart, who ran a Dance Congress in New York, invited us to teach at her convention in June over a three-day weekend. She had heard about us being ex-Sadler's Wells Ballet dancers and wanted us to teach a ballet. At first Mrs. C. refused to let us go, but finally gave in when we convinced her we had to make some money. As it was, we had to borrow money from a friend to pay for our flight to New York. Prior to going, we decided to teach *Coppélia*. So Richard and I spent endless hours writing out three acts of *Coppélia* in our own method of notation, which we sent to Stoddart to copy for the teachers and dancers attending her convention.

At the Dance Congress, we got through an act a day and it moved along successfully despite one funny moment when Richard was at the microphone explaining the steps I was demonstrating from the notes. But we were not in sync. So he blurted out, "You're f_____ing me up", not realizing the microphone was on. While in New York, we joined Janet Roughton (Fred Franklin's one-time secretary) to go and see the Slavenska-Franklin Ballet in Westport, Connecticut. We enjoyed the program, especially the opportunity to see Fred perform again and then afterwards. Another pleasure was seeing him dance with guest artist Alexandra Danilova. The next day Danilova called our room. It so happened that we were staying in the same hotel. Richard answered the phone, and she implored, "Deek, come to my room for a while. I would love to see you." Richard had always been Dick . Everybody called him Dick. But when he met me, he asked me to call him Richard, which I have always done.

When Danilova and Fred were guest artists with the Sadler's Wells Ballet in 1948, Richard played Benno, the Prince's friend in the second act of *Le Lac des Cygnes* and partnered Danilova briefly at the end of the *pas de deux*. We went to see Danilova and had a lovely visit.

Once back in Chicago, we decided to find a place of our own, but we didn't want a Murphy bed. Luckily we found a four-floor walk up on Hyde Park Boulevard, opposite the Piccadilly movie theatre. It was charming and attic-like, with a sloping roof. We had a bedroom, living room, kitchen and bathroom, and we could walk out onto an upper-level back porch, which wrapped around two sides of the building. We bought our furniture at the Salvation Army, and some of these items are still in our possession. We loved having our own little haven.

We gradually got together enough good students to put together a program of *divertissements,* including a couple of *pas de deux*, which we performed on occasions: at the Chicago Arts Club, the opening of the Ogden School on North Dearborn Street and at the Conrad Hilton Hotel for a dinner in honor of the visit of H.M. Queen Elizabeth to Chicago.

3. Audrey Hepburn.

Other events helped alleviate the tension at the school. Audrey Hepburn came to Chicago to appear as Gigi in the play of that name. Through the recommendation of the British Consul, Berkley Gage, Audrey came to class at our studio on a fairly regular basis, about three times a week, except for one day when she sent us a note, regretting having to miss her class "for purely feminine reasons". Richard wouldn't let me teach the morning class if she was there. She was a beautiful dancer, with a head and back similar to Fonteyn's. We became friends and, on Christmas Day, Berkley Gage invited Audrey and us to his home. We arrived just in time for Her Majesty's Christmas Day speech; so the four of us sat listening to the radio—very patriotic. Others joined us later, including my cousin, Michael Evans, who was in the cast of *Gigi*, adding to the pleasure of the occasion.

Members of other professional shows came to class, *Pal Joey* and *Guys and Dolls* dancers, including Deedee Woods and Don Lurio. And actors were with us for quite a few weeks at a time. Julie Harris came to class when she was in town.

Talking of stage stars, before we left England, Richard and I helped in some small way to get Mary Martin's daughter, Heller, into the Sadler's Wells Ballet School while her mother was appearing in *South Pacific* in London. Mary told us, before we left for Chicago, to look up her good friend Mrs. Loyal Davis. We did, and she invited us to a private screening of *The Winning Team,* starring Ronald Reagan—a favorite actor of ours—who was married to Mrs. Davis' daughter, Nancy Davis.

Another altercation with Mrs. C. occurred when Lucille Stoddart invited us to New York to teach for her Congress again. We overcame that problem and went to New York in July 1953. This time, we taught excerpts from the second act of *The Nutcracker*.

In Chicago, some talented students were attending our classes. One such student, Dom Orejudos, came as a beginner and immediately showed ability and a quick and intelligent mind. In a short time, he showed an obvious choreographic talent when he arranged a few delightful dances.

In early 1954, the Sadler's Wells Ballet performed in Chicago, the first time since we left the company. It was wonderful to see them again. They rehearsed at our studio and used a few of our students as supers, which caused much excitement on their part.

Some of our close company friends made their way to the South Side and climbed the four flights of stairs to visit us in our little apartment. We made Frederick Ashton his favorite cheesecake.

The Royal Winnipeg Ballet was also in Chicago in early 1954, and company members came to class at our school. Betty Oliphant, the director, took us to lunch, at which time she asked us to consider coming to Winnipeg as artistic directors of the company. We explained to her about the difficulties at the Allegro School, but told her we probably could get out of our contract. It seemed the answer to our problems. So after careful consideration and advice from our lawyer, we wrote to Betty accepting her offer. But it was not meant to be. Shortly after, the company's headquarters suffered a disastrous fire, putting an end to our plans.

Meanwhile, things went from bad to worse with Mrs. C. She had formed a small board with herself as president. It also consisted of Richard, two other people who supported us, and her lawyer. At this point, she was communicating only by means of notes and letters, one of which was a list of 12 mostly ridiculous dos and don'ts. She was determined to have complete control and again refused to let us teach for Stoddart. Things came to a head, and she fired Richard. She expected me to stay!

Richard and I began to pack our belongings and prepared to leave, much to the shock of the students—most of whom gathered their things and left with us. But Mrs. C. had locked some students in a dressing room. We left with her screaming that she was going to call the police.

So we and the students were out on the sidewalk, along with costumes, books, music, typewriter and sewing machine. We waited until the students were safely on their way home or their parents had arived to meet them, telling them we would be in touch. As we were about to hail a taxi home, our neighbors Ken Johnson and Neal Kayan drove up, surprised at the situation. They drove us home.

The next morning Ben and Sylvia Black, the parents of one of our students, Bonnie Black, called to say they would like to discuss setting us set up in a school of our own. They were wonderful and did just that, and we named it the Ellis-Du Boulay School of Ballet.

We found temporary quarters near the old Charmets restaurant at Michigan and Chicago Avenues and informed our students. Meanwhile we searched for permanent space, which we found at 20 West Jackson Boulevard in the Great Northern Theatre Building. The space was comprised of seven partitioned offices and, with the help of one young man, we tore down most of the partitions with a sledge hammer, venting our fury at Mrs. C. with each blow. We created a nice-sized studio, two dressing rooms, a reception area and an office. We put mirrors along one wall. But adhering to our training at Sadler's Wells, we did not have the students face the mirror during center exercises. Looking in the mirror made their heads move rigidly in an effort to see their reflection, instead of using the attractive nuances of head movements so important for a graceful dancer. Also, we always said that there would be no mirrors for them to look in once they stepped on stage.

When we started our own school, we were able to follow the guidelines we had always insisted on and which had been a bone of contention with Mrs. C.—in particular the grading of classes, which she did not approve of because she believed it was not money making. We didn't care, as we were sure it was the only way to properly train students.

We also insisted on a uniform for each level of classes as an incentive to students eager to reach a higher grade or "color". We stuck to these ideals throughout our teaching days.

We also gave our students a thorough knowledge of the terminology and meaning of the steps of ballet, which we found sadly lacking in the majority of cases. We offered ballet theory classes. We also were appalled at the poor training some students had been given before they came to us. Many were being allowed to go on pointe too soon. Some of the new students and their parents would complain when we took them off pointe until they became stronger. To these complaints, we said "Take it or leave it." Most took it.

Our syllabus continued to be the one both of us had been used to at Sadler's Wells. To our minds, it was the best because it incorporated the better elements of the three major schools of ballet: the Russian (Vaganova), the French (Royal Academy of Dancing), and the Italian (Cecchetti).

There was a time when I first became a professional dancer that I thought teaching would be the last thing I'd ever want to do. Yet as soon as I tried it, I began to really like it and eventually love it. I learned so much myself in the process, as analyzing students' work made me do the same with my own.

People asked Richard and me why we didn't continue to perform. We both agreed that we wanted to give our full attention to teaching ballet. We felt we could not do both, each were full-time professions.

4. Ellis-Du Boulay School of Ballet.

On May 21, 1954, the Ellis-Du Boulay School of Ballet was incorporated, with Ben and Sylvia Black, Richard and me as directors. Classes commenced in our new studio in June.

It was a busy time. We went to the Stoddart Dance Congress one more time and taught *Les Sylphides*. We were being advertised as the "Crystal-Clear Ellises". Evidently, our notation was fairly lucid. Subsequently, for sometime after, we met teachers who had used our notes and said how good and helpful they were—except for one teacher who, we heard later, taught her group *Les Sylphides* from our notes. When it came to the "Prelude" solo, which is danced to two repeats of the music, she misread the notes and somehow managed to fit the whole dance into the first time. Richard was asked to produce *Coppélia* for Butler University Dance Department in Indianapolis, and we wrote a book on partnering, titled *Partnering—The Fundamentals of Pas de Deux*, with an introduction by our good friend Frederic Franklin and published later that year by the Ballet Book Shop. Ballet Book Shop was located on the floor above our studio and run by a dear older lady, Edna Lucille Baum. We spent many hours in her shop and became good friends with her and her assistant, Rod Quiros. I wish there was still such a place.

5. Meeting Robert Joffrey.

Our association with Indianapolis continued for a few years, when we were asked to be on a panel of judges for the Margaret Sear Scholarship Fund. Margaret had been a member of the Sadler's Wells Ballet and on our American tours, where she met a member of our touring orchestra, a violinist with the Indianapolis Symphony. They married, and Margaret started teaching ballet at Butler University in Indianapolis. Then tragedy struck. Eric Rosenthal, her husband, was driving with her on an icy road when the car skidded and crashed, killing Margaret. Months later, he set up a scholarship fund for ballet dancers in her name. Eric wanted us to be judges for the first auditions. Also on the panel were P.W. Manchester (also English), co-editor of *Dance News* and Robert Joffrey. It was our first meeting with him.

Robert, Richard and I were the scholarship judges for another two years. During this time, Robert told us of the plans he and Gerald Arpino had for establishing a small touring ballet company. In January 1957, we attended the Joffrey Ballet's first performance in Chicago at 8th Street Theatre, and then all subsequent visits.

In 1955 we moved to 859 North Dearborn Street. We were delighted with our new home. We still had stairs to climb, but only three floors this time. The rooms were bigger, and there was a working fireplace, high ceilings and a fire escape with enough room for a table and chairs. The kitchen, though, was so small that if the oven door was open, you couldn't get in or out. There was only one very narrow working shelf, so when I wanted to make pastry, I had to put foil on the floor and roll it out there.

We did all the teaching and running of our school, with Mrs. Black's help in the office. We tried to take Sundays off for a little relaxation, which usually meant bowling with Eric Braun, a former principal dancer of Ballet Theatre whom we had met in New York when we were on tour, and was now living in Chicago.

During our summer break, Richard and I drove to Daytona Beach, our first of many visits to Florida.

6. School Classes.

Also in 1955, we offered a successful teacher's course, which we repeated for the next three years.

One of the qualities I consider most important for a teacher to possess is patience. It is a definite asset, and one must have a thorough knowledge of one's profession because, as students progress, most become discerning. Unless you know all the answers regarding their class work, you lose their respect. Of course, if you don't train them to be discerning by stimulating their minds as well as their bodies, they won't be motivated to reason or ask questions. So a teacher must never stop learning, It is hard to teach unless you love it. It's too much hard work unless you do.

Because we insisted on strict grading, sometimes the classes were small. Grading was done on talent, not age necessarily. We had eight divisions, three for children from the age of seven; two for adult and teenage beginners; two levels of Intermediate students; and an Advanced class. The Intermediate I level had to attend a minimum of three classes per week; the next level of four classes per week; and the Advanced at least five a week, not including extra classes, such as character, *pas de deux*, variations and, for a while, classical mime.

Mime was not taught in many ballet schools here. Most of our students enjoyed the class, and I would have continued to teach it. But with the changing times and economics, and being limited to one studio, we had to eliminate mime.

We did have the pleasure of meeting one of the greatest mimes of our times, Marcel Marceau, while he was appearing at the Great Northern Theatre in 1958. After seeing his opening performance, a friend introduced us to him and we all went out to have a drink. We sat and talked literally until dawn. What a wonderful artist and fascinating personality. We made sure to see his subsequent performances.

In our Variations class, which we offered weekly, I not only taught solo dances but some *corps de ballet* works: the "Garland Dance" from *The Sleeping Beauty*, the "Waltz of the Flowers" from *The Nutcracker*, etc. Prior to leaving the Sadler's Wells Ballet, I had written down most of the steps and floor patterns of the classical ballets.

The Ballet Guild of Chicago invited us to participate in its annual performance, which included other Chicago dance schools. We contributed two numbers the first time: a ballet choreographed by Dom Orejudos, *The August Witch*, and a *pas de trois* from his ballet, *A la Foire*. We performed for the Ballet Guild for about three years.

Also in 1955, we opened a small branch of our school in Highland Park, with one of our advanced dancers teaching most of the classes. It never really worked, I think, because neither Richard nor I could spend time there. So after a while, we sold the school to Eric Braun, who ran it until his untimely death.

Richard wrote to Frederick Ashton in 1956, asking his permission for us to stage *Les Patineurs* and *Façade*, which he did. So we rehearsed *Les Patineurs,* and the students gave an excellent showing of it in the studio.

Dom continued to choreograph and was working on *Thais* (music by Franz Liszt). Hy Somers, another of our students and promising choreographer, was rehearsing his ballet, *Alborado del Gracioso* (music by Maurice Ravel). And I kept busy making costumes.

I also was getting involved in the Benesh Dance Notation. John Field had told me about it on one of the Sadler's Wells Ballet visits and had asked Joan Benesh to send me further information about the method. Joan and her husband Rudolph Benesh, who was a musician, invented this system. Joan had been in the company for a while before I left. She sent me some material, and I was intrigued by the very logical concept. I started to take a correspondence course, which was not easy since any questions I wanted to ask meant writing to Joan in London and waiting for replies. No e-mail in those days. My test papers also went back and forth. But, eventually, Joan said I was ready to take the test to obtain a teacher's certificate. Christopher Newton was coming to Chicago with the Royal Ballet in the near future and was qualified to test me. This is what happened, and I received a teaching certificate, which gave me authorization to teach solo work. I taught Benesh Notation to a small group of students, whom I'm afraid didn't keep it up for too long, except for Dom and another young choreographer/student named George Montague (who later changed his name to Montaigne). Both of them continued to use the Benesh Notation for their ballets.

7. Performances at St. Alphonsus Theatre. First Visit Back To England.

With three promising choreographers and a lot of talented dancers in the school, we gave serious thought to putting on a small program at the St. Alphonus Church Auditorium (later known as the Athenaeum Theatre).

We prepared for two performances, which were presented April 13 and 14, 1957. The program consisted of Hy's *Alborado del Gracioso*; *Thais* by Dom; the "Grand Pas de Deux" from *Don Quixote,* which Frederic Franklin taught Richard and me; and our arrangement of *Casse-Noisette (The Nutcracker)* Act II.

Pamela Johnson and John Prinz, as young students in our school, played Clara and the Nutcracker Prince in *Casse-Noisette.* They were among eight of the 25 dancers in that program who would later join major ballet companies. Pamela became a soloist with the Joffrey Ballet, and John a principal with American Ballet Theatre.

At the end of the summer term, we returned to England to visit my mother and Hil. My mother helped pay our fare, as we were still hard up. She and Hil had moved from Ealing and bought a house in Cross-in-Hand in Sussex, not too far from Brighton and the Sussex Downs, which I loved so much. The two-story house was called Garden Cottage, part of a large estate named Possingworth Park. My mother and Hil, both avid gardeners, turned what was a small wilderness into a beautiful garden of winding paths and tiered levels, a rock garden, herbaceous border and flowering trees and shrubs. The charming brick house was partially covered in roses and wisteria.

It also was roomy, with three bedrooms upstairs and a big bathroom with a shower (a luxury then). Downstairs there was a dining room, a kitchen and a comfortable living room with a fireplace. The kitchen, though, was not that big. So when Richard and I stayed there, it was a bit crowded. I suggested putting up a one-way sign to help us move around the center table. But they did have a refrigerator, albeit a very small one. My mother had to clear out some things to make way for ice trays to supply enough ice cubes for the two "Americans," who now required ice in their drinks.

We delighted, too, in Garden Cottage's proximity to Brighton, where we drove on quite a few occasions through the charming town of Lewes. In Brighton, we spent many hours browsing for antiques in the famous "Lanes," sometimes buying little items. We spent a few days in London, staying with Denis, who was now living in Cadogan Gardens near Sloane Square.

In 1958 we acquired an agent, who secured a few dates for our small group of dancers. One was in St. Joseph, Michigan, with the Twin Cities Orchestra in the High School Auditorium. By this time, we decided to call our company the Illinois Ballet and applied for a charter from the State of Illinois for official registration, which we received in December 1958.

Earlier in the year, the Sadler's Wells Ballet (now the Royal Ballet) performed at the Civic Opera House again, and we confirmed with Ashton about producing *Façade.*

That year my cousin, Michael Evans, came to Chicago in a production of *My Fair Lady* at the Schubert Theatre. He was playing Professor Higgins, and Anne Rogers was Eliza Doolittle. After the first performance, we were invited by the British Consul to a cast party. On arriving at his house, someone came up behind me and said, "Hello cousin Christine." It was Michael. I really didn't know him well, but we had a delightful meeting and discussed our various family members.

Some years later, I happened to be watching "The Young and the Restless" on TV, and there was Michael. He had a part on the soap opera for quite a few years and portrayed a retired English colonel, a good friend of "Victor Newman's". I managed to find Michael's address in Hollywood and wrote to him, mentioning the fact that he always wore a cravat, which is Richard's trade mark. He wrote back saying he only wore the cravat for his TV role; otherwise, he was a sweater-and-jeans man. He also said that he had remarried, and his wife was an ex-ballet dancer who knew of us.

Myself with students: Penny Tall, Pamela Johnson, John Prinz.

Façade, "Popular Song" with Larry Long, Richard.

Façade, Ruth Ann Koesun, Dom Orejudos.

Snow White on TV. Richard (second from left), Dom Orejudos, Elisabeth Herskind.

One In Five, Dom Orejudos, Frank Spolar, Richard Peterson, Hy Somers, Elisabeth Herskind.

Coppélia, Richard as Dr. Coppélius.   *The Nutcracker*, Richard as Herr Drosselmeyer.

Pas de Quatre on WTTW TV.

Chapter VII
Illinois Ballet: 1959-1970

1. Formation of Company. Studio Move. *Façade.*

We started making plans for the Illinois Ballet's first performances in early 1959, and on April 10th, we opened at the St. Alphonsus Theatre at Lincoln, Wellington and Southport. Two more performances were given on April 11th and 12th. On opening night, our nerves were heightened when the stage manager, William Ploeger, called for the fire curtain to be raised but it wouldn't budge. This procedure was usually done by a hydraulic system, which had failed. Richard and I became frantic, but Bill endeared himself to us as he calmly, with some assistance, raised the fire curtain by hand. Twenty minutes later, the performance began.

A la Foire was the first ballet, which was about spectators at a fair; characters included the Strong Man, the Bearded Lady, the Balloon Seller and Clowns. The music was by Dimitri Shostakovitch, costumes by Dom and set design by William Schermer, a local artist.

The "Pas de Deux" from *Don Quixote* followed, with Anna Marie Longtin and Frank Spolar.

Next came *Arabesques*, an abstract ballet by Eric Braun, which he had first produced for the Ballet Guild of Chicago, with music by Mozart and new costumes by Dom. Eric performed in his ballet, dancing the *pas de trois* with Bonnie Black and Alexandra Nadal.

We used the arrangement by Frederick Ashton for our presentation of "Florestan and his Two Sisters" from *The Sleeping Beauty* Act III, with Carol Flemming, Alexandra Nadal and Richard Zelens. *Coppélia* Act III closed each performance. Eric, as Franz, partnered Bonnie Black as Swanilda in the *pas de deux*. We followed these first performances with three more at the St. Alphonsus Theatre on June 19th, 20th and 21st, repeating Dom's ballet *Thais* with costumes by Dom and set design by William Shermer. Dom used a two-scene synopsis. The first tells of Thais and her attendants engaged in a bacchanal, which is interrupted by the arrival of Paphnutius, a young monk who has come to Thebes to save the beautiful Thais from her sinful ways. She is so overcome by the religious zeal of the young monk that she leaves with him to enter a convent. On the way, at the beginning of the second scene, she collapses from fatigue. Paphnutius realizes his interest in her is no longer spiritual and tries to make love to her. She refuses to yield to him and, in her exhausted state, dies.

We also repeated Hy's ballet, *Alborado del Gracioso*, and added another excerpt from the classical ballet repertoire, the "Pas de Trois" from *Swan Lake* with Bonnie Black, Alexandra Nadal and Richard Tarzynski. Whenever possible, we used live piano music performed by William Hughes and Donald Miller.

We heard rumors that the Great Northern Theatre building was scheduled to be torn down to make way for a new building. In 1959, we got a notice to that effect. We were upset for two reasons: one, we would have to move and, secondly, we hated to see a theatre razed. So we had to search for new quarters. We found good space a block away at 20 E. Jackson.

The new space needed little work. It was on the seventh floor, and there was only one other tenant on that floor—a dentist. I remember when Richard was putting up the barres in the studio, he accidentally drilled through to the dentist's office. We hoped there wasn't a patient there at the time—two drillings would be a bit much to take. We had a dressing room of our own, a large office, two dressing rooms for the students and another room we made into the wardrobe for the ever-mounting number of costumes.

With Dom and Hy full of ideas for ballets, our repertoire continued to grow, making it possible to involve as much local talent as possible.

There was not much time after our move to prepare for our next program at the St. Alphonsus Theatre on September 25th, 26th and 27[th,] where we premiered a new ballet by Dom, *This Persistent Image*. It had a psychological theme involving a young girl, her parents, her unhappy relationship with them (especially her mother), her attraction to the lodger (who was the mother's lover) and the demon, who beset her in the form of her image in the mirror.

Anna Marie Longtin created the role of the girl; Joseph Nelson was her father; I her mother; Hy Somers the lodger; and Christina Niezabitowski her image.

The music was to some of Sergei Prokofiev's *Visione Fugitive*. Dom designed the costumes and William Schermer the stark set, which included the mirror and two high-backed chairs for the father and mother.

Those performances were highlighted by the premiere performance by an American ballet company of Frederick Ashton's *Façade*. Dom had designed a new set and costumes. Eric Braun and Richard were wonderful in the "Popular Song"—two pros having a good time.

2. St. Alphonsus Theatre.

Talking of pros, we were so fortunate to work at the St. Alphonsus Theatre as there was a "built-in" stage manager, William Ploeger. Bill was wonderful and a pro, and I think he admired the fact that Richard knew about the theatre and its workings after his experiences at the Royal Opera House. Richard and Bill got on very well, and Bill did so much for us. Besides his heroics on our opening night, he helped build and paint scenery, and he could make any theatre workable—as we were to find out when we encountered ill-equipped stages on our tours. Bill usually came with us.

We loved working at the St. Alphonsus Theatre—an atmospheric vintage place, with a good- sized stage and proscenium opening, fairly good wing space, a fly system and downstairs dressing rooms.

But there were a few drawbacks in those days, particularly the theatre's location, which was considered "off-Loop". Therefore, critics seldom attended our performances. Our only reviews were those written by dance critic Ann Barzel, who—for whatever reason—didn't seem too enthused about our company. The stage had a poor surface, one that today's dancers would refuse to dance on unless a special floor covering were laid down. We had no such thing, so all we could do was paint the stage before each series of programs to help smooth the splintered surface. This could not be done until all the dancers had left after the final rehearsal. Then Richard, Bill and I would set to and paint the stage. Occasionally one of the priests from St. Alphonsus Church next door would come over with welcome refreshments. One more drawback was the lack of decent restaurants or ones that stayed open late in the vicinity of the theatre. That meant we had to drive all the way south on Lincoln Avenue and beyond before we could find a nice restaurant. Nowadays there are more than enough, but Richard and I—tired and hungry—had quite a long way to go before we found somewhere to drown our sorrows in food and drink.

3. Expanding Repertoire.

In November, Illinois Ballet gave its first downtown performance at the Goodman Theatre. It was just one performance, but we got an encouraging review from Donald Hennahan in the *Sun-Times*.

We finished up the year by premiering two movements of a new ballet by Hy Somers, *Valse Promenade*, at New Trier High School Auditorium in Winnetka. *Valse Promenade* was an abstract ballet to music by Mikhail Glinka, with a *corps de ballet* of six girls and two boys, and two soloists danced by Alexandra Nadal and Dom Orejudos. Alexandra, or Sandy as we called her, later married Eugene Slavin of the Ballet Russe de Monte Carlo and, together, they directed the Austin Ballet for many years.

Also on the New Trier program was *This Persistent Image*, with Ruth Ann Koesun as the Girl. Ruth Ann, a principal soloist with Ballet Theatre, was now living in Chicago, her home town. She happily agreed to be a guest artist at some performances with Illinois Ballet. She danced the role of the Debutante in *Façade*, and the Girl in *This Persistent Image*, adding her expertise to the performances and delighting us all.

Early in 1960, Hy completed *Valse Promenade*, adding a third movement that he placed between the first two. It was to the lovely Second Movement of Vasily Kalinnokov's *First Symphony*, which involved two couples and the *corps de ballet*. It was performed for the first time on February 14th at St. Alphonsus—now officially renamed the Athenaeum Theatre.

Hy's next ambitious work, *The Moor of Venice*, used music from two Richard Strauss compositions. James Estes designed the handsome costumes and effective set. Richard Peterson created the role of the Moor, and Joyce Baker was his wife. Dom was an Ensign in the Service of the Moor, and Richard a Captain in the Service of the Moor. I was the

Ensign's wife, Elisabeth (Betsy) Herskind was the Captain's mistress. Birute Barodicaite and Linda Phillips completed the cast as servants.

It premiered on June 25th. When the curtain came down, there was an absolute hush. Then the audience started applauding loudly. It appeared to be a success.

Dom's *Pas de Deux Classique* to music by Sergei Shostakovitch also premiered on that date and was performed by Barbara Macklem and Hy Somers.

We seemed to have a penchant for producing ballets an act or two at a time. In this case, it was Dom's latest creation of *Snow White*, and he started with the third act. It was set to selections of music by Edvard Grieg and part of the June 25th program. The cast included Snow White, Prince Charming, the Wicked Queen, the Good Fairy, seven woodsmen instead of dwarves (Richard was one of them after a few performances), and six wood nymphs.

In July, our agent got us a date in Lakeside, Ohio, our first out of state—followed by one in Remington, Indiana, a Chataqua program.

For all these early tours we rented a U-Haul trailer, which we hitched to our Buick to carry the costumes, scenery and lighting equipment. Richard did the driving, with me in front as the navigator. Bill Ploeger and Margaret Corre, my wardrobe assistant, sat in the back. It is strange to think back on those days. There were some expressways, but not as many as now, with fewer trucks. We had no seat belts, air bags or air conditioning.

We used the Buick until one New Year's Eve, while celebrating at a friend's house on the North Side. We had parked the car nearby. During the party, we heard a huge bang. Looking out, we discovered the bang was our car. It had been sideswiped, and the culprit was nowhere in sight. The car never fully recovered, so we got a more practical station wagon instead. With its big roof rack, we were able to do without a trailer most of the time.

4. Civic Theatre Performance.

We had become friends with Merrill Shepard, a well-known lawyer and patron of the arts, and his wife Brenda, an actress who used her maiden name of Forbes. She was English, and her brother was Ralph Forbes, also on the stage. Merrill and Brenda had been very encouraging about our company, and we talked about a fundraising board.

We planned to do a performance at the Civic Theatre, the small replica of the Civic Opera House next door. Merrill suggested he invite some people who might be willing to support us.

Up until now, we had been using pianists or reel-to-reel tapes for our musical accompaniment. On this occasion, we decided our equipment was not good enough for the Civic. So we borrowed sound equipment from a friend of a friend.

The advanced bookings for the performance, which was on October 8th, 1960, were good thanks to Merrill's efforts. We did advance publicity as far as our meager budget would allow. As it turned out, it was about the worst time of our lives. From the beginning, the sound was awful—due mostly to our inexperience in sound equipment. The borrowed set had dirty heads, and we had no back-up system. But we completed the program, which included *Valse Promenade, The Moor of Venice* and the last act of *Snow White*.

Merrill arranged for some of his friends to go back to his house for a small party afterwards to meet us (Brenda was away on tour). When we arrived, there was no one except Merrill. It was devastating, and he had been so helpful.

Most people thought we were through and would call it quits. But they didn't know us. We refused to give up and were determined to continue with our goals: to encourage and give an outlet to dancers and designers, and not to resort to leotards and bare stages. We were rewarded by an "angel" who gave us new sound equipment. The dancers rallied behind us, which was quite wonderful since they were virtually unpaid. Most of them had full- or part-time jobs, and a few were still in high school or college. Because of this, nearly all our dates were on the weekends and so were most of our rehearsals. The dancers were given their pointe shoes, ballet shoes, character shoes, and all costumes and tights when we were performing and also any lodging or transport that was necessary. We were so fortunate to have such dedicated dancers over the years.

We were also committed to another out-of-town date, this one in Benton Harbor, Michigan, on October 30th.

During the year, Dom completed the first two acts of *Snow White* and, on December 3[rd,] we premiered it at the Athenaeum Theatre. Richard Chen, a local artist, designed the two striking sets on painted stage cloths, which were executed by our talented Bill Ploeger. As so often, Dom designed the costumes. It was the first full-length original ballet by an American choreographer in many years. Unfortunately, nothing was made of that fact.

5. Ray Powell's *One in Five*. WTTW Programs.

The Sadler's Wells Ballet came again to the Opera House at the end of 1960 and into the early days of 1961. During this visit, our good friend Ray Powell offered us his ballet, *One in Five*, which he had choreographed originally for the Sunday Ballet Club in London in 1960—a generous gift and a boost to the company. Ray came to the studio and taught the ballet in three days. Derek Rencher, who had designed the original costumes and sets, kindly gave us sketches of these for us to work from.

The ballet is about five clowns, all dressed alike. Gradually four of them realize that one is a girl. Ray chose music by Johann and Josef Strauss, and it was set on a bare stage, except for one tall ladder and one shorter one, a wide piece of red cloth hung by ropes and a large wicker basket. The original cast was Elisabeth Herskind, Dom Orejudos, Frank Spolar, Hy Somers and Richard Peterson.

1961 was to be a busy year. We were planning to stage *Le Spectre de la Rose*, with Dom as the Spectre and Ruth Ann Koesun as the young woman. Unfortunately,

Dom developed hepatitis and was unable to perform for some weeks—thus, we shelved *Spectre*.

So for the first time we presented our production of the "Grand Pas de Deux" from *The Sleeping Beauty*, with Michelle Lynn and Hy Somers, as part of our program at the Athenaeum on February 18th.

In early March, we set off on tour again to Wittenberg College in Springfield, Ohio.

Then on March 18th, we gave the first performance in the States of Ray Powell's *One in Five* at the Athenaeum. As always, we sent invitations to the press. Claudia Cassidy replied and sent her regrets, explaining she could not attend because she had to review a Van Clybourn concert. Tough! She wished us luck with the Powell ballet.

Earlier, we had been approached by WTTW-Channel 11, Chicago's PBS-TV station, to do a half-hour program as part of its *Festival* series, with Jim McPharlin as director. We decided to present *This Persistent Image* and the *The Sleeping Beauty* "Pas de Deux" for the television program, which was filmed live at the Channel 11-WTTW studio at the Museum of Science and Industry on March 30th.

Then we provided the dancers for a production of *La Traviata* by the Chicago Park District Opera Guild and toured again—four times in Indiana in four different towns: Collegeville, Remington, Fort Wayne and Indianapolis.

On July 6th, we did a second program for Channel 11 with *A La Foire* and a *pas de deux*, titled *Encounter*, by George Montaigne to music by Paul Creston. And we were scheduled for one more TV program with Jim McPharlin on September 25th at the Museum, this with *Snow White*. Michael Loewenstein, Channel 11's resident set designer, produced marvelous sets despite the extremely small studio space. Like the others, this was a live performance. Sadly, we have no record of those early TV productions, just a few stills. In those days, tapes were made but eventually discarded.

In September we returned to our "home," the Athenaeum, and added another ballet by Dom to our repertoire, *The Stone Medusa*, with music by Heitor Villa-Lobos. The dramatic piece depicted a sculptor who creates a statue of the mythical Medusa. He tires after the effort and falls asleep in a chair. He awakens to find the statue has come to life and begins to be seduced by her. But, in the end, she kills him with her snake. Elisabeth Herskind created the role of Medusa; Dom the sculptor.

6. Larry Long. Dance Critics.

Meanwhile Larry Long, who was a soloist with Ruth Page's Chicago Ballet company, had come to class with us a few times. We asked him if he would like to dance with Illinois Ballet, if he could obtain permission. He said he would love to. Thus, started lengthy correspondence between us, Ruth Page, AGMA, Carol Fox (as Ruth's company was appearing with Lyric Opera) and Ardis Krainik. Happily, Larry was allowed to perform with us for a series of three weekend programs at the Hinsdale

Community House. He appeared in the *Don Quixote* "Pas de Deux" with Elisabeth Herskind and the "Popular Song" in *Façade* with Richard. We really enjoyed having him with us.

In October, we were asked by Ak-Sar-Ben to be part of the Ak-Sar-Ben coronation ceremony in Omaha, Nebraska, appearing as the "Royal Ballet." Richard and I were flown to Omaha to discuss this with "the powers that be" and Joseph Levine, who was the musical director and conductor. It was such a pleasure for us, as he had been conductor with Ballet Theatre. We decided to do a version of *Valse Promenade*, using extra dancers for this event. All went well, and we performed before Illinois Ballet's largest audience.

One last program that year took place at the Studebaker Theatre in Chicago's Fine Arts Building on December 3ʳᵈ, with a new production of *Thais*. We invited Larry Long to dance with us again, but too many stumbling blocks got in our way, Regretfully, we had to cancel his appearances. We had the feeling that we were a possible threat to Ruth and her company. But none of this lessened our admiration and fondness for Ruth.

On Christmas Day, WTTW aired *Snow White* again.

In February 1962 we made a frigid trip to Columbus, Ohio, where the company was appearing at Capital University, and we met up with A.V. Coton, the English dance critic, who was visiting the States to comment on dance here.

He volunteered after the performance to return to Chicago with us on the bus—a brave soul, since there was ice inside the windows. He subsequently commended the Illinois Ballet in *Dance and Dancers'* magazine in May 1962. We also knew English dance critic P.W. Manchester, who wrote about ballet before she moved to New York, where she was co-editor of *Dance News* with Anatole Chujoy and co-author with him of *The Dance Encyclopedia*. "Bill", as everyone called her, stayed with us on a few occasions when we were living on Dearborn Street. She was an avid baseball fan. And it was she, an English woman, who taught us about the game, which we have enjoyed ever since and have become Cubs fans.

Throughout the year, we added three more works to our repertoire. George (Montague) Montaigne produced a ballet for us called *Con Gioco*: a carefree piece for five girls and two boys using excerpts from Ernst Dohnany's *Variations on a Nursery Song*.

Richard and I staged the "Blue Bird Pas de Deux" from *The Sleeping Beauty* with Pamela Johnson and Dom Orejudos. Since the time Pam appeared as little Clara in *Casse-Noisette*, she developed into an excellent dancer with a strong technique and lovely stage presence.

The third work Dom had originally set for the Washington Ballet earlier in the year, called *Memento*: a light, romantic ballet with excepts from music by Georges Bizet. These works premiered on October 6ᵗʰ at the Athenaeum Theatre.

The company also performed in five different Chicago suburbs, with the Lithuanian Opera Company in *Aida* and in Mandel Hall at the University of Chicago.

7. Kirov and Bolshoi Ballets. Touring.

London's Royal Ballet, the Royal Winnipeg Ballet, the Kirov and Bolshoi companies came to Chicago in 1962.

The Kirov used our studio for company classes, which were mostly taught by Natalie Dudinskaya, and made us realize where the dancers got their strength. Some of the Russian dancers were intrigued with the school library in our office and spent time perusing our books, especially ones that referred to Rudolf Nureyev, since they probably had little knowledge of his life after his defection from the Soviet Union.

The Bolshoi also held classes in our studio, taught by the wonderful Asaf Messerer. But we remember being horrified seeing Maya Plisetskaya do *grand pliés* in second position and going way down beyond the horizontal line of her thighs. That was something we had been told never to do, and we taught our students never to do. But we loved watching the dancers rehearse small segments of *pas de deux*, especially when the delightful Leonid Lavrovsky was dancing.

In 1962, Dom was approached by Dan Jordan, a student of Human Development. For his doctoral thesis, he was interested in examinig the role of non-verbal experience in psychological health and theorized that ballet might assist in assessing patients with psychological problems.

Dan worked out a synopsis and wrote a score. He hoped Dom and the Illinois Ballet would be willing to produce it with help from his research grant. Dom choreographed the ballet, called *Metamorphosis of the Owls*. Its first performance, which drew much publicity and a full house, was at Mandel Hall on October 13th, 1962. Two more performances at Mandel Hall were well attended—all of which helped pull the company out of the red.

The *Chicago Tribune* did a large article about our production of *Owls* in the Sunday Magazine, with a photo of Michelle Lynn on the cover. We were happy about that.

Soon after this, Fred Franklin came to Chicago with the Washington Ballet, which he was directing at the time. He came to our studio and saw Michelle and was impressed with her work. He asked her to join the Washington Ballet, which she did. It was hard for us when some of our especially talented dancers left our company. All the same, it was rewarding to know we had helped them on their way.

In early 1963, the Evanston Symphony Orchestra—conducted by Frank Miller, principal cellist of the Chicago Symphony Orchestra—invited the Illinois Ballet to perform with them. It was a pleasure and an honor to work with Frank.

In April, we presented *Dances from Les Sylphides* using only the four soloists—no *corps de ballet*—which worked out quite well.

We toured Cedar Falls, Iowa and Madison, Wisconsin, then stayed in Chicago for a while.

That year we all lived through the shocking news of President Kennedy's assassination. On that fateful day, Richard was teaching morning class. I had just gone across the road to the bookstore on the corner of Jackson and Wabash when I heard the news on the shop's radio. I rushed back to the studio and told Richard the news. He stopped class and spoke to the students. We canceled the rest of class and all others for the day, as well as the day of the funeral. Richard and I stayed at home that day and watched the television with our neighbor—a moment in history we shall never forget.

On December 22nd, we presented the condensed two-act version of *Snow White*. In that program, I appeared off-pointe as the Wicked Queen. An amusing incident occurred at one performance. In the first act I was seated, looking very imperious on a large throne, with my elbows resting on the arms. Suddenly, one of the arms fell off the throne, letting my arm fall limply—just as four dancers were approaching me. It was all we could do not to break up.

I enjoyed my role, especially in the second act for which part of my costume was a wide, long cloak. I made the cloak by piecing together large patches of shimmering, multicolored fabrics. They had been part of a few huge boxes of fabrics that a relative of one of our students had given to me. He was in the fabric trade, and these were unneeded remnants. I was thrilled to have so much material during those financially strapped days. We designed several costumes around the various remnants. There were even pieces of fur, which were used in *The Moor of Venice*.

In early 1964, the Fort Wayne Civic Ballet sponsored a performance by the Illinois Ballet. In April, we went to Racine, Wisconsin, and did another program with the Evanston Symphony Orchestra conducted by Frank Miller.

Our autumn program at the Athenaeum, included more excerpts from the classical repertoire. We staged the "Peasant Pas de Deux" from *Giselle* Act I and *Coppélia* Act II.

Richard was marvelous in the role of Dr. Coppélius; Pamela Johnson a spirited Swanilda; and Dom an ideal Franz.

We stayed in Chicago for most of the year. During this time, a couple who offered to help us with public relations, John Cofoid and his wife Barbara Ome, prepared a proposal to send to various granting organizations. We had some substantial endorsements from Dame Ninette de Valois, Sir Frederick Ashton, Merrill Shepard, Frank Miller and Daggett Harvey. Despite this, we got negative replies from all, except the Sears Roebuck Foundation, which gave us a small but much-appreciated grant in early 1965.

In a 1965 article in the *Chicago American*, dance critic Ann Barzel commented on our Sears Roebuck grant, inferring that the only good things we did were "snippets" from the classics. She never mentioned the fact that we were the first company here to produce Sir Frederick Ashton's *Façade* and Ray Powell's *One in Five*—or that we were fostering local talent.

John Cofoid wrote to her on our behalf, asking her why she took this stand. But she wrote back insisting she stood by her statement. We were never able to understand Barzel's lack of support for our efforts even if, to quote her, we were "for the most part an amateur group." We never claimed to be wholly professional. We were giving local talent a chance to perform the classics and new ballets.

On January 23rd we had another date in Racine, Wisconsin, for two performances. On our drive back to Chicago, Richard and I hit an ice storm. We decided to make a short stop near Highland Park. When we got back into the station wagon, the brakes were frozen. Somehow Richard managed to get us home safely but, when we got out of the wagon, we found it covered in ice with a thick layer wrapped around the antenna.

We performed around town and appeared twice at the Athenaeum, once in March and once in October, when we premiered another ballet by Dom, *Fifth and Briefest Season*.

We went to England during our summer break. My mother took us to Chichester in Sussex to see Sir Laurence Olivier in *Othello*. What a treat! He was magnificent. Added to our pleasure, a friend of ours from Ireland, Joyce Redman, also was in the cast playing the part of Emilia. We had a nice reunion with her.

In December, Ruth Page presented her lavish new production of *The Nutcracker* — sponsored by the Chicago Tribune Charities—at the Civic Opera House. Ruth invited Richard's old friend and mentor, Anton Dolin, to be Herr Drosselmeyer.

WTTW-Channel 11 again asked us to tape a half-hour program for its *Facet* series. On January 26th, 1966 we did the second act of *Coppélia* using our own set. Pamela Johnson was Swanilda; Dom was Franz; Richard was Dr. Coppélius.

This was to be among the last times Pam appeared with the Illinois Ballet. Robert Joffrey saw her at one of our Athenaeum Theatre programs and invited her to join the Joffrey Ballet. We missed her, but were happy for her. Three of our original dancers had also been in the Joffrey Ballet: Anna Marie Longtin, Joe Nelson and Richard Zelens.

The Lithuanian Opera Company produced *La Traviata*, and we provided the dancers. For three weekends in April and May, we performed under the auspices of the Illinois Arts Council in Elk Grove.

We had another date in Omaha. Richard went ahead in the station wagon filled with costumes and scenery, accompanied by Dom's brother Gil. On the way they had a flat tire, which meant unloading everything inside the wagon out onto the shoulder to get to the spare. Looking back, we laughed to think of the reaction of the passersby seeing this weird collection of furniture on the side of the road. The rest of us traveled by bus.

The Northwest Symphony Orchestra booked us for a performance in Des Plaines in November. Our other out-of-town date was in Galesburg, Illinois. We did only one performance at the Athenaeum in 1966.

Anton Dolin returned again in December to appear in Ruth's *The Nutcracker*. We decided to ask him for his permission to stage his *Pas de Quatre*. He agreed with three stipulations: 1) We were to pay him royalties for each performance. 2) Ruth Ann Koesun must put it on for us. 3) We must try and get the Danish recording of Cesare Pugni's score. We happily agreed to all of this.

8. Arson Attempt On Studio. Lecture-Demonstrations.

That year, we had a traumatic experience. There was an arson attempt in our studio at 20 E. Jackson. We had been rehearsing Saturday evenings and Sunday mornings. The janitor used to let us in on Sundays. We told the dancers they could have one particular weekend off and informed the janitor that we would not be in on Sunday. Richard and I were enjoying a nice long sleep when the phone rang. It was the janitor asking if we knew anything about the gasoline drums in the studio. We said we had no idea what he meant. He insisted we come down and see for ourselves. Now horrified and wide awake, we dressed, flew out of our building, got a cab and arrived at the studio in the fastest time ever. When we stepped out of the elevator, we saw a row of five-gallon containers full of gasoline propped at an angle against the stairwell banister. All the caps were off, and there were more around the corner by the utility closet. In the studio itself, we found the floor covered with gasoline-soaked newspapers. More tilted and open containers were positioned throughout our space. In all, there were nine five-gallon drums and six three-gallon drums, along with two phone books on the studio floor (one badly charred) and a huge swatch of matches. A portion of the studio floor was charred, where someone had tried to burn the phone book.

We immediately called 911, and soon the firemen and police were on the spot. Even though it was a cold day, we had to open all the windows to let out the nauseating smell of gasoline. Soon the "top brass" from the fire, police and arson squads arrived. They asked us a lot of questions, and our answers seemed to convince them that we knew nothing of how this had happened. We told them about a suspicious-looking man we had seen for some time carrying large cardboard boxes into the building.

The head of the arson squad told us that whoever set this up was not a professional arsonist. If he or she had been, our building and many in the block might have been seriously damaged. But the plot failed because the alleged arsonist tried to set the fire in a large area—our studio—instead of a small one, which would have been more combustible. The head of the arson squad advised us to move out of the building, since he believed this person would most likely try again. He was right. Some time later, there was another unsuccessful arson attempt on a higher floor.

Richard and I did most of the work for the school and the company. We planned the programs and cast the ballets (with the choreographer's approval), did program layouts, and arranged for the printing of these and advertising flyers.

We received a mailing permit, which meant coordinating the bulk mailing that, when ready, was taken to be mailed. All this took quite a while, most of it being done after the last class of the day.

Richard was in charge of the office and book work, which entailed a daily check of attendance and billing. We devised a fool-proof system of checking all of this, but it was a time-consuming job. At the end of the month, Sylvia Black balanced our bank book and worked out all the taxes. This, long before the days of computers and cell phones.

Richard also taught all levels of classes, except the children. I taught all levels, including the variations class. We did have good help. I had two mothers who tackled all the tedious work in the wardrobe, and one of them came on tour with us.

John Cofoid and his wife Barbara Ome helped greatly with public relations. For a while Rod Quiros, whom we had met at Ballet Book Shop, served as general manager. He was followed by Leon Bram, another Ballet Book Shop devotee, and Bill Ploeger, our stage manager.

From the beginning, we decided against having a board of any sort. Our philosophy was "Mother, I'd rather do it myself."

The year 1967 got off to a busy start, with a performance at Ball State University in Muncie, Indiana, followed the next day at the Horwich Centre in Rogers Park, Chicago.

The Illinois Arts Council co-sponsored two performances in Elk Grove. On January 24th, we had a terrific snow storm, which is now in the history books. Richard and I drove downtown and parked in an indoor parking lot near the studio. It had started to snow heavily by early afternoon, so we decided to cancel classes after many phone calls from students saying they would be unable to get in. Only one student turned up. Her mother had driven her all the way from Waukegan—talk about dedication.

Richard and I finally left the studio. Seeing how slippery it was, we decided to leave the car and take the subway home to Chicago Avenue. From the station, we had to walk three blocks home—quite an obstacle course. At one point, Richard and I fell down in a mountain of snow and just lay there laughing. There had been 23 inches of snowfall that day, snarling traffic for days.

The next day, we went outside on Dearborn Street and looked downtown—it was a white world, absolutely deserted. Walking to State Street for some food, we went along Chestnut Street where the snow was piled up to shoulder height.

But we felt we ought to get to the studio, where we got quite a bit of work done with no interruptions and no classes. Hy Somers and George Montaigne turned up, and said nobody else would be open except us.

In May, we premiered two new ballets at the Athenaeum. Dom and Hy both choreographed new works. Dom's ballet was called *Spanish Suite... and Short* set to selections from music by Leon Minkus and Francois Auber, with Peggy Powell and Dom in the lead roles and a *corps de ballet* of six girls and two boys.

Hy's ballet was *Pélleas and Mélisande* to the Jan Sibelius score. Birute Barodicaite was Mélisande, and George Montaigne was Pélleas. Both choreographers designed the costumes for their own ballets.

The costumes for the *corps* girls in *Spanish* were very effective, consisting of wide short skirts of layered net. We did a trial run of the ballet at the Woodstock Opera House on April 29th. The stage was so small, the girls had barely enough room to move in their costumes.

Meanwhile the Chicago Board of Education, with a grant received under Title III, engaged the Illinois Ballet to do lecture-demonstrations at a number of Chicago high schools. The first of these was on October 13th, and the last on December 13th. The Board of Education gave us our itinerary of two schools a day, 30 performances in all. Richard and the Illinois Ballet dancers, Peggy Powell, Birute Barodicaite, Juanita Lopez, Suzi Kirby and Dom Orejudos, piled into the station wagon with costumes and sound equipment.

They left early in the morning with my map of their route and returned early afternoon. I stayed at the studio and held down the fort. They were usually greeted by a school official who, when Richard announced they were the Illinois Ballet, invariably replied, "Oh, Illinois Bell."

The lecture began with Richard introducing himself and the company. The dancers then performed the lively opening section of *Spanish*, which we hoped would catch the students' attention. It was followed by a short educational section describing, with demonstrations, the seven movements of ballet, which are *plier* (to bend); *tendre* (to stretch); *glisser* (to glide); *relever* (to rise); *tourner* (to turn); *élancer* (to dart); and *sauter* (to jump). Then we showed how ballet can tell a story, with an excerpt from *A La Foire* and *This Persistent Image*. An explanation of classical ballet was shown with the opening of the *Don Quixote* "Pas de Deux". The program closed with the last section of *Spanish*.

Richard asked the audience, after the educational section, to try and pick out some of the movements that had been discussed. The program was, overall, well received—except for an occasion in one school when someone released tear gas. The dancers quickly found an exit and some fresh air.

9. Fine Arts Building. Anton Dolin's *Pas de Quatre*. WTTW *Chicago Festival* Programs

In 1967, we regretfully left 20 E. Jackson Blvd., after finding a studio on the top floor of the gorgeous old Fine Arts Building on Michigan Avenue, with a lovely view across Grant Park to Lake Michigan. We installed the barres, making them level with the floor. But when we lined them up with the horizon, something wasn't level. The dear old building was evidently slightly off center.

Many famous dancers came to that studio; its proximity to the Auditorium Theatre made it very convenient. We remember well watching the historic theatre being restored. We were thrilled to see it being used again. But we and many others were disappointed that local artists had not been invited to perform at the grand opening of the theatre. Instead, the New York City Ballet appeared in George Balanchine's *A Midsummer Night's Dream*, in our opinion, not one of his best works. But the wonders of the theatre's acoustics were well demonstrated when Norman Ross, announcing the occasion, refused a microphone and every word was clearly heard.

Margot Fonteyn, Rudolf Nureyev, Natalia Makarova, Eric Bruhn, Ivan Nagy, Bruce Marks and many more came to the studio to rehearse or to take class with us. A couple of times, Eric Bruhn asked if he could use the studio and gave a private class to some of the American Ballet Theatre dancers during a time when the company was performing at the Auditorium Theatre.

Eric was, in our estimation, the epitome of the classical *premier danseur*, a true *danseur noble*. It was exciting to watch his classes. Nureyev attended every one. I remember one amazing moment when Nureyev was standing in the center of the studio in his famous tight fifth position from which he then did a *developpé* to a perfect second position without twisting his hips or moving his supporting foot—difficult to do.

Prior to our leaving 20 E. Jackson, we received a call from Richard Carter, one of the directors at WTTW-Channel 11. He wanted to discuss the possibility of our doing another program for them, this time for their *Chicago Festival* series. Richard (Dick) Carter came to see us at the studio. We got on so well and had a very productive meeting. We decided that excerpts from *Spanish Suite ... and Short*, with Daiva Gustautus and Samyiel Kurkjian dancing the leads, were to be part of the program for Channel 11. We completed the half hour with *The Stone Medusa*, with Daiva as the Medusa. The TV programs were no longer live, but taped to be shown at a later date. Thus, this program was filmed and then aired on October 3rd, 1967. Jack Summers was executive producer and Dick Carter the director.

During the year, we were going ahead with our plan to stage *Pas de Quatre* after receiving Dolin's approval. We contacted Ruth Ann Koesun, who agreed to set the ballet for us. She had worked with us before and had danced in the *Pas de Quatre* with Ballet Theatre.

After some time, we were able to obtain a copy of the Danish recording of the Pugni music from James Eaton at Harkness House. It was much better tempo-wise and more complete than the Richard Bonynge recording.

Rehearsals went well, Ruth Ann was marvelous, and the girls worked hard to perfect the special period style of the ballet, which portrays four dancers as ballerinas of the mid-19th century. Birute was cast as Taglioni; Juanita as Grahn; Suzi as Grizi; and Peggy as Cerito. I enjoyed the challenge of making the costumes and tried to make them as correct as possible, with the help of photographs and lithographs.

Jack Summers and Dick Carter were pleased with the first program we had done for the *Chicago Festival* series, and immediately asked us if we would do another one. We were delighted and chose *Coppélia* Act II. This time, Michael Lowenstein designed a magical set. Richard was Dr. Coppélius; Dom was Franz; Daiva was Swanilda. *Coppélia* aired on December 19th, 1967. It subsequently won a NET award for Excellence in Cultural Programming for Channel 11, which greatly pleased all concerned.

Whenever the Joffrey Ballet came to Chicago, we would nearly always arrange a late buffet supper for Robert and Gerald Arpino, some company members and close friends. The first time I prepared an English trifle for dessert and, thereafter, Robert said he would come to see us only if we served trifle. He always wrote delightful thank-you notes.

It was in 1967, on one of their visits, that Robert told us he had seen Sir Frederick Ashton in London and asked him if the company could stage *Façade*. Fred had received a knighthood in 1962. Fred hesitated and did not give his approval. Robert hoped that, if Richard agreed to put it on, it might sway Fred's opinion. Richard said he would be delighted to do it. It was left that Robert would talk to Fred again when the Royal Ballet came on its next visit to the States in June. But Fred didn't come with them. Gerald Arpino wrote to Richard on Robert's behalf asking Richard to write to Fred and try to get his approval for the Joffrey Ballet to do *Façade*, which Richard did.

After much negotiating, Fred finally agreed as long as Richard would rehearse it, stage it, and John Hart would supervise the final rehearsals and casting.

Pas de Quatre was given its first performance by Illinois Ballet at the Athenaeum Theatre on March 9th, 1968 with some very nice advance publicity.

Bill Ploeger suggested projecting a picture of the original lithograph onto a screen, which would fade out as soon as the dancers began to move. It worked beautifully.

Also on the program was the premiere of *Vivaldi Variants*, choreographed by Hy Somers. Working on this ballet had been a therapy session, as Hy had been through a disturbing period when he tried to commit suicide by taking an overdose of aspirin. He was lodging at Bill Ploeger and Phil Kania's house. Fortunately Bill found him in time, and he was rushed to the hospital where he recovered. We persuaded Hy to return to work on his ballet, hoping it would help—which it did for a while. He left soon after completing *Vivaldi Variants* and returned home to Idaho. The next time we saw Hy, he was in Duluth, Minnesota working with George Montaigne, director of the Duluth Ballet. A few years later, though, we heard that Hy committed suicide. What a waste. He was very talented, a good dancer and an excellent partner. His was a sad, troubled and too-short life.

The WTTW-*Chicago Festival* production of *Coppélia* Act II was slated to be shown nationally on April 4th, 1968. But it was taken off the air midway with the breaking news of the assassination of Martin Luther King.

Following Dr. King's death, violent riots and fires broke out in various areas of Chicago. We realized the severity of the time while sitting in the restaurant on the ground floor of the Park Hyatt Hotel at Michigan and Chicago Avenues with friends. We saw army vehicles drive by full of soldiers with bayonets drawn—not a sight we expected to see in Chicago. It was very disturbing.

10. First Color Program on WTTW. Visit to Europe. Lou Conte.

Dick Carter called us and was very excited because General Electric offered to loan Channel 11 a color camera for a short time. He wondered if we could get a ballet program together in time. We were happy with the idea, too, and Dom was just putting the finishing touches on a new ballet, *The Charioteer*, with music by Samuel Barber. This work and *Pas de Quatre* paired well and were the right length for the half-hour program. So we filmed the two works at the WTTW studio. They aired on October 1st.

Meanwhile, Richard had received a letter from Andre Eglevsky asking him if he would stage *Coppélia* for his company. After some exchange of letters, plans fell through. Richard and I, however, staged the full *Coppélia* for the Grand Rapids Ballet in Michigan when Sally Seven was the director. Sally had been in the Ballet Russe de Monte Carlo and the Slavenska- Franklin Ballet. Richard did the first and second acts; I did the third.

Then we staged it again for Joseph Savino, who also had been in the Ballet Russe de Monte Carlo and was director of the ballet company in St. Paul, Minnesota. This time, Richard did only the second act; I the third; and Fred Franklin the first—talk about combined operations.

In August, Richard and I flew to England and stayed in London with Denis in the house where he was working in Cadogan Gardens. We drove to Sandwich, Kent and stayed a few days with my father and Jane. While watching the news with them one evening, we were shocked at the scenes of rioting in Grant Park during the Democratic National Convention being held in Chicago, with occasional shots of the Fine Arts Building. How odd were the circumstances.

An amusing item about Sandwich. I have a photo that I took of a signpost outside the town of Sandwich—one part is directed to Ham and another to Sandwich. Talking of signposts, we often tell of the time we were driving in Devon and came to a sign that pointed to Puddleton. Further on, one said to Piddle Hinton and, finally, one to Piss Hill.

Every time we returned to England, we saw my mother in Sussex. I also tried to see two of my aunts and my cousin Jane Bond, who has become a well-known portraitist and lives in London in a darling little house not too far from Olympia. Jane was born in Umtali, Southern Rhodesia, but later moved to London with her parents. She started her artistic career designing costumes and sets for films and the stage. Then she became a portrait painter and has had many exhibitions of her works, which are also in private collections in Europe and the United States. My Aunt Alison and her friend Stella MacDonald had bought a lovely thatched house right on the cliffs near Hastings—a secluded spot we visited a couple of times. After Stella died, Alison moved to a compound of houses for retired people in Winchester. For a while, my Aunt Peggy was living in a flat in Knightsbridge in London. She had enough room for us to stay, which we did, until she moved to Winchester to live with her sister.

From England, we flew to Portugal for the first time and stayed in Estoril for a week. We loved what we saw of Portugal, including the food, even in the most remote restaurants.

We went to our first bullfight, which was an experience. The Portuguese do not kill the bull, only stun him with picadors. The toreadors looked so handsome riding on horseback. Even after the bull is stunned, there was still a lot of fight left in him. Then an army of men try to subdue him—a hard job but, in the end, they win.

Starting on October 15th, Richard and five dancers gave a second series of lecture-demonstrations for the Board of Education—40 in all.

Dom was replaced this time by Lou Conte, who was a student of ours then. We were trying to persuade Lou to become a classical ballet dancer, because he was so talented and had the ideal physique. But he eventually returned to his first love, jazz, and founded and directed the now-famous Hubbard Street Dance Chicago. The lecture-demonstrations concluded on November 22nd.

11. Richard stages *Façade* for Joffrey Ballet. Decision to Close Illinois Ballet. Visit to Europe.

The time had come for *Façade* to be staged. Richard flew to Albuquerque to meet the Joffrey dancers and decide on the casting of *Façade*. The company was performing in Albuquerque, where Richard met Basil Thompson, Joffrey's ballet master, for the first time.

Basil had been with the Royal Ballet since 1952, and then immigrated to the States. There is a story that, when Basil was leaving his hometown of Newcastle to join the Sadler's Wells School of Ballet, he had been told by a friend who had been an officer in the Royal Navy with Richard, to be sure and ask for Richard Ellis when he got to the Opera House. Basil did so, only to be told that Richard Ellis had left for America the day before. They finally met and became good friends.

Richard returned to Chicago and then went to New York in December for rehearsals of *Façade,* with a few days off to return home for Christmas.

WTTW re-ran the color program in December.

Returning to New York to continue rehearsals, Richard arrived at the studio to find that tragedy had struck with the untimely death of dancer Maximilian Zomosa. The company was stunned. Max had been slated to dance the Tango in *Façade*. So his role as the Gigolo had to be recast. Richard wanted Basil for the role, but Joffrey's final decision came down to Luis Fuentes. Robert was in full agreement with Richard that Pamela Johnson should dance the Polka, which was ideally suited to her. She had performed it with us in our Illinois Ballet production of *Façade*.

John (Jack) Hart came to New York at Fred's request to supervise the final rehearsals. Jack condescendingly said that what Richard had done was right, except for a few things which he changed. Basil always backed Richard up, saying he was right. After all, Richard had been in *Façade* long before Jack.

The Joffrey Ballet was scheduled to appear at the Auditorium Theatre in Chicago in January. Due to the death of Maximilian Zomosa, the company canceled the ballet *Astarte*, in which he was the principal male dancer, and programmed *Façade* instead. Thus, the first performance by the Joffrey Ballet of *Façade* was on January

28th, 1969. Its New York premiere wasn't until February. Unfortunately, Richard was unable to be there.

Illinois Ballet appeared in another *Chicago Festival* program in January, this time along with a local singer, once more directed by Dick Carter. The program was titled *Viva Canto*.

In March, the company was back at the Athenaeum with the first stage performance of *Charioteer* and the premiere of Dom's new ballet, *Songs of a Wayfarer*, to the Mahler music of the same name.

In May, the company traveled by bus to Duluth at the invitation of George Montague (he had changed his name again).

Viva Canto was re-run in June.

For our holiday that year, Richard and I went to Puerto Rico for the first time. Freddie Franklin was there, so we had fun. One day, we took a trip with him to St. Thomas and had a wonderful time. On our return flight to San Juan, we were told that the plane was air-conditioned. We thought, "How nice." It turned out to be three or four small fans.

We filmed another program for Channel 11 and again Dick Carter directed. The ballet we chose was *Pèlleas and Mèlisande*. It aired on October 7th.

In May 1970, we gave what were to be the last performances of the Illinois Ballet at the Athenaeum Theatre. Two programs on May 2nd and 3rd included *The Stone Medusa*, *Pas de Quatre*, *Songs of a Wayfarer* and *Coppélia* Act II, with Peggy Powell as Swanilda.

Things were getting increasingly difficult as far as the company was concerned, money being the main factor. Bill Ploeger suffered from diabetes and was hinting that he ought to go a little easier. He had a permanent job, which was his priority. The principal dancers were interested in more permanent work, which we couldn't give them unless we became a full-time professional ballet company—something we were not up to. Leon Bram, who was such a staunch supporter and guide, was leaving for a new job in New York. In addition, we felt some of our regular school students were of the opinion that we neglected them for the company and/or wondered why they were not chosen to be in the company. So, all in all, we decided sadly to call it quits.

In August, Richard and I returned to England and stayed with Denis in London. While we were there, we saw the Kirov Ballet at Festival Hall. The *Don Quixote* "Pas de Deux" was on the program, with a young (unknown to us) male dancer Mikhail Baryshnikov. We were impressed. But we were not impressed with the company's presentation of Anton Dolin's *Pas de Quatre*. The cast included Natalia Makarova. We thought it was miscast and seemed of the wrong period, with heart-shaped bodices and large puffed sleeves. How Dolin allowed that, we do not know. He was in the audience with Wendy Toye, and we spoke to them briefly. We thought better of voicing our opinions.

It was not long after this appearance of the Kirov that Makarova and Baryshnikov defected.

After London, Richard and I went to see my mother and Hil in Sussex. From there, we went to Spain for our first visit and stayed in a delightful little hotel near Marbella and a short walk to the beach. As usual, we rented a small car to visit more places in the vicinity.

While in Marbella, we saw an announcement for a bull fight. We purchased tickets when we saw that the famous El Cordobés was to appear, along with two other toreros.

In Spain they try to kill the bull, which is distressing. But, nonetheless, the spectacle was an experience. The first two toreadors were very good and quick to the kill. El Cordobés was not so quick, perhaps wishing to extend his performance. And perform he did. His looks and his actions reminded us, in many ways, of Nureyev. He knew where the cameras were and played to them to perfection.

Another day, we decided to go to Tangiers. There was a special daily trip by bus to Algercieras and then a hovercraft to Tangiers. When we disembarked, we were told to stay as a group, especially in the Casbah, keeping in mind how it was depicted in the old-time movies. We toured a little of the city and were so interested to see Eastern architecture. We watched snake charmers, too. On the way back to Spain, we had a good view of the famous Rock of Gibraltar, which I had seen so many years before on my way to Palestine.

On our way back to London, we spent a couple of days in Madrid, delighting in a visit to the Prado.

When we got to Heathrow, security was very tight due to the recent and one of the first hijackings. While we were at the passport check, the man at the desk, seeing that our English passports were issued in Chicago, turned to another and said laughingly, "Hey, we have a couple of defectors here."

Chapter VIII
1970-1976

1. Richard in Ruth Page's *The Nutcracker*.

Ruth Page had been searching unsuccessfully for a replacement for Anton Dolin, who was not returning after four seasons in the role of Herr Drosselmeyer in *The Nutcracker*. Why she didn't approach Richard in the first place is something of a mystery. His background and the fact that he lived in Chicago made him a natural choice. But in 1970 she eventually asked him, and he agreed—delighted at the thought of being on "the boards" again.

When it came time for Richard to start learning the role, Larry Long—who was now Ruth's chief assistant—gave Richard a video of a performance with Dolin in the role. However, most of the scenes with Herr Drosselmeyer were so dark in the film it was almost impossible to decipher what he was doing. Plus, Richard did not want to copy Dolin's interpretation. He wanted to create his own. This concerned him greatly until one day, Richard hit upon a characterization he felt comfortable with and one that enabled him to get into the role.

He didn't have his first rehearsals with the company until late October. This was a bit nervewracking, since Richard had not been given much guidance. He continued to do his best but, frankly, he was a little perturbed by Ruth's lack of encouragement. He got the feeling that she seemed to believe only her original cast was any good. But Richard persevered. Then, during the first stage rehearsal, matters changed.

Sam Leve, the production's designer, was on stage with Ruth watching Richard when he turned to Ruth and said to her, "You know Ruth, this man is so much better as Drosselmeyer than Dolin." Thereafter, Ruth continued to praise Richard's performances—as did so many others.

The production took place at the Arie Crown Theatre at McCormick Place, which had reopened after a disastrous fire. It was a big and unfriendly auditorium, but it held many people.

The cast of the first production with Richard as Herr Drosselmeyer also included Violette Verdy as the Sugar Plum Fairy and Helgi Tomassen as her Cavalier. Six members of Illinois Ballet were also in the cast.

The last program of that season fell on New Year's Eve. We had made prior plans to fly to Las Vegas with our good friends Rod Quiros and Vince Saviano. Richard did not appear in the second act at that time, and took his curtain call at the end of the first act. This fact, combined with the time change, enabled us to get to Las Vegas before midnight. So off to O'Hare we went and flew to Las Vegas. From the time we walked into the terminal, we were laughing at the sight of row after row of slot machines before one ever got to a casino.

We stayed at the Stardust Hotel, partly because my cousin Jillian and her husband Mitch were in *Le Lido de Paris* at the Stardust. Jillian, or Jilly as we call her, was — like her cousin Jane — born in Umtali, Southern Rhodesia, where she attended a local dance school. When she was 15, it was decided that she was good enough to further her studies in England, which she did. But being a little too tall for ballet, she went into some shows in London and, from there, to a show in Paris. This led to work in Las Vegas, where she met her husband Mitch, who was also appearing at the Stardust. Jillian had arranged for us to have a table to see the lounge show and be at the New Year's celebration there. It was a marvelous show, added to which we realized that one of the dancers was Judy Chelle, a former student. She suddenly saw us but covered her shock very well. Afterwards, she joined us for a while.

The next day we went to Jilly's home and met Mitch for the first time.

That evening we saw *Le Lido de Paris,* with her in the wonderful nude adagio act she did with her partner.

We also spent a little time in the casino before returning to Chicago and the studio.

2. Illinois Ballet's Last TV Program.

Illinois Ballet was committed to one last date on April 25th, 1971 in St. Joseph, Michigan. How strange that one of our first out-of-town dates was in St. Joseph's twin city of Benton Harbor; stranger still, that at a later date, we would buy a house nearby.

Dick Carter wanted us to do another TV program. This time we chose *This Persistent Image*, with Peggy Powell, Diane Vrettos, Dom, Richard and me in the cast, and excerpts from *Valse Fantasie*, as we called it then, with Elisabeth Herskind and Dom in the lead roles, and Franca Barchiesi, Heidi Ellison, Penny Jay, Jocelyn Lorenz, Nancy Mikota and Roberta Pfeil in the *corps*. It was another color program, and Michael Loewenstein designed attractive sets. The program aired on June 29th. In August, Channel 11 re-ran *Pélleas and Mélisande*.

In September, Dom and Betsy performed a *pas de deux* from *Snow White* as part of a program for WTTW. Illinois Ballet's last television appearance for Channel 11 was a re-run of the June program, and this program won three local Emmy Awards for the station. The National Academy of Television Arts and Sciences awarded Michael Loewenstein an Emmy for the scenic designs for Illinois Ballet, and Dick Carter received an Emmy for the same program and for other *Chicago Festival* shows.

So we can say that we bowed out in a blaze of glory.

All in all, Illinois Ballet appeared 21 times on Channel 11-WTTW.

The company had also been the stepping stone for quite a few of our dancers, who went on to join other ballet and dance companies. Many of these dancers received most of their training with us.

Occasionally we invited guest artists to perform with the company and were fortunate to have such well-known dancers as Ruth Ann Koesun, Eric Braun, Ronald Colton, Gildo DiNunzio, Larry Long and Michael Maule. We toured in Illinois, Indiana, Iowa, Michigan, Minnesota, Nebraska, Ohio and Wisconsin, as well as the Chicago area. The company produced 33 works, 20 of which were original choreography for the company, and I made more than 300 costumes.

We've frequently been asked why Chicago was not able to sustain major ballet companies, prior to the Joffrey Ballet making its home here. Ruth Page had a professional ballet company, but it was rarely seen in Chicago. For a while, there was Maria Tallchief's Chicago City Ballet. Over the years, we have sat in on quite a few committee meetings on how to start a ballet company. It always came down to the same answer: not enough funds, too many egos, too many people wanting to start too ambitiously with productions of *The Sleeping Beauty* or *Swan Lake*. No one could agree on the safer and more manageable small company—the way many major ones got their start, government-sponsored companies being the exception. Yet there have been numerous small, non-professional companies, our Illinois Ballet being one of them. Some have been of very high standards and have been excellent launching pads for aspiring dancers, giving them a chance to perform and a taste of what dedication to the art means.

3. St. Tropez.

Working together so often led to a lasting friendship with Dick Carter. We shared many memorable times with him and his friend John MacMillan when they lived in Chicago. John was an excellent cook, and they often invited interesting guests to dinner. On one such occasion, Ruth Page was one of their guests. During dinner, Richard turned to Ruth and asked her, "Could we possibly beg, borrow or steal your house in St. Tropez?" We had heard so much about it from other friends. She immediately replied, "Of course, darling. If I am not there, the place is yours." The outcome was we did go to St. Tropez and stayed at "Herbe Folle" (the name of Ruth's house) in August 1971. Ruth wrote lengthy and amusing instructions for us.

Because we were the first guests who ever had to close up the house, naturally Ruth was concerned and had many instructions.

They came in a used envelope with crossed-out personal reminders on one side and our names and "Welcome to St. T" on the other. Underneath was scribbled a message: "D'Henry said he will water the plants in the courtyard, but if he doesn't will you? I hope the new man will be good."

Inside the envelope, we found two long pages all in Ruth's scrawly handwriting, some in blue ink, some in red ink and most in pencil, full of instructions obviously written at odd times as she remembered certain things.

I now quote:

> Please turn off electricity (in chest outside near swing).
>
> Be careful to use doorstops as the wind comes up suddenly and doors and windows slam and the glass breaks easily and you can never get it fixed! The seashells in the living room are doorstops.
>
> Please turn off both iceboxes (house and studio).
>
> Telephone doesn't work unless you jiggle the part that holds the receiver.
>
> Be sure to bring the white cushions in at night (from the terrace).
>
> Please water the garden everyday. You may not need to, but the gardener usually doesn't come till after the house is closed.
>
> To close the shutters in the studio you have to tie it with rope.
>
> I don't think the oven works. The gardener may grease it as I will not.
>
> Put the wooden statue on table in courtyard inside before you leave.
>
> Wash your feet in bucket in outside toilet because if you get sand in the shower no one will come to fix it.
>
> Leave outside gate unlocked because the garbage man comes 3 x a week at 5 a.m.
>
> Be sure to always lock house and studio when you go out as there are a lot of thieves around.
>
> Simone or Morisette clean for me every day for 2 or 3 hours but does no cooking. I pay 5 francs an hour.
>
> Simone Antoine will be the caretaker of the house but she has a new baby so is no help now.
>
> Simone does all the laundry. She lives near Clavés.
>
> Jean D'Henry is the man who takes the garbage and he can probably take all the furniture in etc., but he is brand new so I don't know how good he will be.
>
> I have always been careful myself to close the house and it is hard to tell anyone what to do.
>
> You can give the keys to Simone Antoine (she lives just beyond Clavés) and then give the key to the gate to D'Henry.

This place is a lot of trouble. But lots of fun and I do hope you will enjoy it. Am so sorry not to be there. Have a good time.

Much love. R.P.F.

You have to put the garbage in the big can in the back of the house.

Please eat and drink anything that is left over here.

There are clean sheets on all 3 beds.

I closed the apartment over the studios as I think the house is more comfortable.

We drink the water from the faucet.

Don't throw out the empty tin box—we use it for bread or crackers.

White chairs in courtyard go into the studio.

I think my new gardener will take the swing in as he is new. I am not sure what he will do.

The Clavés that Ruth mentions were the artist Antoni and his family. Clavé had designed sets and costumes for quite a few ballets by Roland Petit and also for Ruth. Another neighbor of hers was Brigitte Bardot. One day, Richard and I walked to her place and around her swimming pool. She was not at home; in fact, nobody was around.

To get to St. Tropez the first time, we flew from Chicago to Paris and then took a train to St. Raphael, where we picked up a rental care and drove the lovely drive to St. Tropez, which could be reached only by bike, bus, car or boat. When we arrived, we had a little trouble finding the sign for the road to Ruth's place. Suddenly, while driving around the Place des Lices, I spotted the name among many others on the side of a building. Eventually, we got to Herbe Folle. We then drove on up the road to Simone's house, and she gave us the key. Back we went and opened the double doors into the courtyard. On the left stood the main two-story building, and on the right, a smaller building with the studio on the ground floor and a small apartment above it.

We toured the house and found a balcony upstairs with a lovely view of St. Tropez Bay.

After settling in, we went into town and strolled around St. Tropez. One of the chief delights of this charming place was a building code that allowed no tall buildings, such as some of the high rises that have spoiled the beauty of much of the French Riviera.

Being sun lovers, we found our way to the famous beaches that are quite a long drive from town but well worth it. The very long stretch of beach is called Pampalon, and all along are sections with different names, like Plage de Soleil and Tahiti. Most sections have a bar and a restaurant on the beach. And, of course, they're topless beaches. But in those surroundings, it all seemed natural, and the children were so well behaved.

Ruth agreed that we could invite two friends to join us for a while. So Michael Jervis, an Australian whom we had met in Chicago, and his then-wife Patricia stayed with us for a few days. We had a good time, enjoying the beach; the delights of the various streets; and gazing in awe at the size of the luxurious yachts anchored in the harbor. Many of the occupants were enjoying lunch or dinner on the afterdeck, being served by members of the crew. What a life!

We spent a few days in Paris before flying back to Chicago.

During his second year as Herr Drosselmeyer, Richard suffered an attack of pleurisy. Ever since I knew him, he smoked Lucky Strikes. Evidently, Bobby Helpmann introduced Richard to the American brand, which they were able to purchase in London. Richard carried an elegant cigarette case and lighter and smoked up to a pack a day. I never smoked, except on rare occasions in self-defense. But pleurisy, performing and smoking did not go well together, and Richard stopped smoking completely—just like that, which made me very happy and relieved.

1972 was a fairly uneventful year, or so it seemed after the hectic years of Illinois Ballet.

The Emmy awards were held on May 9th. Ironically, it was one of the only ones not to be televised due to a strike of some kind.

In August, we returned to Puerto Rico and stayed in a friend's 23rd-floor condo on Luquillo Beach. It was delightful and relaxing, except for one day when the elevators failed. We found this out as we returned from shopping for groceries. So we had to climb 23 floors, bags of food and all. We must have been in good shape in those days. We don't relish the thought of that now.

4. Return to St. Tropez.

Richard and I flew to Paris for a few days in August 1973, where we got in touch with Bruce Merrill whom we had met in Chicago. He was a well-traveled, professional dancer and, at the time, dancing in *le revue* at the Casino de Paris.

We went to see the show, which was produced by Roland Petit; his wife, Renée Jeanmaire, was the enchanting star. When we approached the ticket window, we were quite surprised to find Roland behind it. We were only able to say a few words. Roland had come to Covent Garden in 1950 to stage his ballet, *Ballabile*. This, Ashton's *Scènes de Ballet* and *Symphonic Variations* were the only ballets in the repertoire that I was never cast in.

From Paris we flew to Nice, spending one night in Cannes and then we drove to St. Tropez. Not wanting to impose on Ruth, we searched for somewhere to stay. We found a small hotel near the Place des Lices.

The next day, we decided to try another section of the beach when lo and behold we saw Ruth, Andre Delfau (Ruth's second husband; Tom Fisher had died), Peter Brown and his dog Rosebud. Peter was Ruth's company manager. She invited us to lunch. Later, she and I went swimming together. She was wearing an old leotard and, once in the water, she pulled down her top. This was not unusual in St. Tropez, but what amused me was that her breasts seemed to be made of foam as they floated to the surface.

She inquired where we were staying and then said that she and her guests were expecting to leave in two days. If so, we were welcome to stay in the studio at Herbe Folle. We were happy when she called to say they were leaving and we could move in. We actually liked the studio better than the house. It was cozier and more compact.

A few days later while on our favorite Plage de Soleil, Richard was swimming and heard a couple who were obviously English. So he spoke to them. It appeared that they were staying fairly near Ruth's place with their two young sons. I was introduced to them: Sallie, Paul, Lawrence and Andrew Littleales. They lived in Surrey. They had a boat, so we enjoyed sailing around the bay and to the beach. From then on, we met every day.

A surprise meeting happened one day while we were walking around St. Tropez. We saw Leslie Edwards from the Sadler's Wells Ballet. We spent the day with him at the beach. Then he came back with us to Ruth's place for a while. Another day, we unexpectedly saw Anton Dolin. He was being driven in a convertible and asked the driver to stop. We talked for a few minutes—amazing coincidences, considering all the people in town.

Back in Chicago during Richard's third *Nutcracker,* there was quite a scare. Just as he was summoning from the wings the bed with Clara on it during the Mouse battle, a light standard caught fire and started to burn a wing. The curtain came down and everyone cleared the stage while the fire crew put out the fire.

Fortunately, noone was hurt, and the audience was informed about the incident. The Snow scene was canceled, and they had the option of leaving or waiting for the second act. Most people waited and, all was well.

Also this year, we heard of the tragic and untimely death of John Cranko on a flight back to Germany after a successful tour of the Stuttgart Ballet in America. On that tour, the company performed in Chicago, and John came to see us in the studio. It was good to see him after so long. We always liked John so much when he was a member of the Sadler's Wells Ballet. He and I were invariably cast as couples. I remember *Mam'zelle Angot,* in particular, and the hours we spent learning the fussy steps.

Little did we know what an incredibly gifted choreographer John would become with his masterpieces, such as *Taming of the Shrew, Eugene Onegin* and *Romeo and Juliet.*

5. Our First Cat. My Father. Another Studio Move. School Programs

About a year after moving to our apartment on North Dearborn Street back in 1954, we were coming home one evening and found a kitten underneath the mailbox shelf. How he got there was a mystery, as he was inside the front door.

We picked him up and took him upstairs with us. He was an adorable, short-haired grey with big ears. We fell in love with him but thought we should try to find out if anyone was missing a kitten. From our point of view, happily, no one made a claim. So Sir Grahame Ellis, as we named him, stayed with us until he died in April 1974, aged 20.

One of his greatest delights was eating olives, especially when soaked in gin. He would try to grab the olives out of Richard's martini glass. We have a photo of Sir Grahame, or Gray as we usually called him, attempting to reach the olives with his paw.

If he managed to get one, he would play with it on the floor until it was nice and dusty. Then he would eat the whole thing.

But it was a sad year, as my father also died in 1974. My greatest regret was that I never had the opportunity to know him well. He was tall, handsome and had a brilliant mind. My parents divorced when I was about 10 or 11, and I didn't get to see my father again until I was 15 years old and then very briefly.

When World War II broke out, he was appointed Director of Intelligence, and as such served with the Royal Air Force Delegation and Joint Chiefs of Staff in Washington, D.C. from June 1941 to April 1945. For this service, he was awarded the Legion of Merit, one of the highest awards bestowed on a non-American. While in Washington, he met and married Jane Balke.

On returning to England, he retired from the RAF as Group Captain. He then became a business man, his last job being joint manager and investment manager of the London office of Bache and Co. He retired on February 1st, 1966.

I saw him again briefly after his return to London from Washington. None of these visits were long enough for either of us to get to know each other better.

Then Richard and I moved to the States, and he and Jane bought a house in Sandwich, Kent.

Our visits back to England were few, and we didn't get to Sandwich every time. The last time we saw my father, he was evidently ill, though he showed no signs of it except for the use of a cane. He was buried in Sandwich, and a tree was planted in the town square in his memory.

Jane, whom he adored, stayed on in Sandwich and fulfilled her dream of becoming the Mayor of Sandwich, a post she held for an unusual two terms.

Apparently, when Daddy was still alive, Jane had voiced her wish to become Mayor. Daddy replied that in no way was he going to allow that since he had no wish to be Lady Mayoress!

We went to see Jane after Daddy's death, and she took us to the Sandwich Town Hall. With the Master-of-Arms help, she donned her full regalia for us and sat in her Mayoral seat.

When Daddy was alive, he and Jane used to go to the famous golf club in Sandwich and exchange stories with Ian Fleming, author of the James Bond books, the first of which was depicted on a golf course.

My father made one visit to Chicago during our first years, staying one night in a hotel while on a business trip for Bache and Co. All the time we had together was for a few drinks in a bar near the studio.

My mother, on the other hand, made two visits to Chicago and stayed with us on Dearborn Street. Some of our friends drove her around while we were at work. She thoroughly enjoyed herself and loved Chicago. On her return to England, she told her skeptical friends how lovely Chicago was. Good for her!

Also in 1974, we moved out of the Fine Arts Building because they were raising our rent at the end of our lease. We found studio space in the Stevens Building at 17 North State Street. It was already a ballet studio, having been vacated by Ruth Page's school and company. Before that, dance teacher Edna McRae had used the space.

While in the Fine Arts Building, we were able to hold our annual class demonstrations in Curtiss Hall across from our studio. The class demonstrations were held for the benefit of parents and family who were not, except on few occasions, allowed to watch classes.

The first one featured the Junior II students showing a set barre work, center work and a short dance. The second involved the Junior III, or advanced children's class, who demonstrated more advanced work in the same format. Later in the day, the advanced students performed excerpts from our repertoire. In retrospect, two of these were special: one was when Michael Bjerknes and Heidi Ellison were the *pas de deux* couple in our excerpts from *Les Sylphides*; the second was when we showed *Pas de Quatre* with Franca Barchiesi and Helene Alexopoulos in the cast. These four dancers all went on to join major ballet companies: Michael Bjerknes to Ruth Page's Chicago Ballet, the Houston Ballet, the Joffrey Ballet and the Washington Ballet. Heidi Ellison danced with the San Francisco Ballet and with the Basel Opera Ballet. Franca Barchiesi joined the Stuttgart Ballet. Helene Alexopoulos was the only student we ever accepted into our school under the age of seven. Her mother brought her to us and begged us to take her. We agreed because we detected something very special about her. After ten years with us, she joined Maria Tallchief's Chicago City Ballet and, from there, went to the New York City Ballet, where she became a principal dancer.

After leaving the Fine Arts Building, we gave the annual show in the studio or in the Ruth Page Auditorium. Over the years, these programs included *Swan Lake* Act II corps de ballet, the "Fiancées Dance" from Act III and the "Pas de Trois." From *Giselle*, the Act II Wilis plus the Queen of the Wilis. We did the "Waltz of the Hours" and Swanilda and her friends from *Coppélia*. Aurora and friends from *Sleeping Beauty* Act I, as well as most of the solos from the classical repertoire.

Some years when we were blessed with good male students, we were able to do our excerpts from *Les Sylphides* and the middle movement from *Valse Promenade*. For these programs, we always featured our present students, never ex-ones or professionals.

While we were running our school , parents of teenagers would ask our advice about their child's future. Most were concerned about the dilemma of sending them to college or not. Depending on our view of the child's talent or potential as a professional dancer, we would advise the parents of very talented students to allow them, if the funds were available, two years after graduating from high school to devote their full attention to dance training. Meanwhile, they could take some college courses. At the end of that time, we recommended they assess the situation and perhaps then go to college full-time. It is never too late to do that. Also, if the student is really determined to be a dancer, denying him or her the opportunity can lead to resentment. We told the parents to let them get it out of their system. Although there are colleges that offer dance majors, usually by the time the student has completed the college courses, it is too late to join a company that is typically looking for younger dancers.

6. Caribbean Yacht Trip.

We had planned a different sort of holiday. Rod Quiros, our friend who was a travel agent, arranged for eight of us to charter a yacht sailing down the Caribbean. At the last moment, he got the annoying news that the yacht had been previously booked. But all's well that ends well, as Rod found another yacht that was "dead heading" to Grenada. It was bigger and, better yet, it was going to cost less.

Birute offered to cat-sit for us, as we now had G.T. (Grahame Two), another grey cat that we got immediately after Sir Grahame died. Birute has become one of our "family." She was born in Lithuania and came to live in Chicago with her parents when she was quite young. In her early teens she came to study with us, after which time she was in the Illinois Ballet, Ruth Page's company and also performed in Europe.

We set off for Martinique, where we were to find the *Ring Andersen*, our 112-foot sea-going ketch.

Making a flight connection in New York, we encountered another problem. The airline had overbooked, and we were told to be standbys. But Rod being a travel agent was able to pull a few strings, and we were able to leave as planned. Not only that, but they put us in first class and gave us champagne.

We landed at Fort du France in Martinique and made our way to the harbor. Our first sight of the ketch was exciting. She looked so big and beautiful. We were taken by dinghy out to the ship and met the captain, Jan, and his wife Elyse and the six crew members. So we were going to be 16 on board.

Since we were not sailing immediately, one of our group and I took a local bus—filled with people, children and chickens—to Mount Pelée, the scene of the famous 1902 volcanic eruption. We were fascinated with the museum that housed many of the artifacts that had been salvaged.

We returned to the ship and sailed soon after. Our cabins were large, with two bunks in each. Because we were only traveling a short distance just to get away from Fort du France, we sailed under steam and anchored for the night.

Throughout our 14-day voyage, we were served delicious food, all fresh from the islands and prepared by the cook. Except for two dinners, he never repeated a menu.

We finally set sail on our first morning. What a gorgeous sight to see all the huge sails unfurl. We only wished we could have been in two places at once: one where we were, and one on another boat watching the action from a distance.

Our first stop was Castries, the capital of St. Lucia. While the ship was being refueled, most of us went into town and were amazed to find on the side of a building a huge sign: the Du Boulay Bottling Co.

Next we sailed to Marigot Bay, a beautiful hideaway from where we went to the Pitons, magnificent sugar-loaf twin peaks. The only way to anchor nearby was by a couple of the crew rowing the dinghy into the beach and tying the ketch up to two palm trees.

From there we were on our way to St. Vincent. The captain, knowing that Richard had been in the Royal Navy, asked him if he would like to navigate the ship for a while, which Richard did quite well, much to our delight. We got to St. Vincent, then continued on to Kingstown.

Our next stop was Bequia, where we enjoyed a lovely beach and beautiful Caribbean waters.

From Bequia, we went to Mustique, where Princess Margaret had a house. The scenery and coloring got more magnificent the further south we sailed.

While sailing around the small islands, we heard warnings that the season's first hurricane was headed in our direction. The weather certainly was getting worse, and the captain made contingency plans. We were to stay on an island, while he rode out the storm on the *Ring*.

The hurricane hit Trinidad but, apart from the threatening clouds and rough water, we were all fine and able to sail again the next day for the Tobago Cays: four tiny islands completely deserted except for the rocks, sand and crabs. After we anchored, the men wanted to go one way and the ladies wanted to go scuba diving, which was not to my liking. I left the dinghy, waded ashore to one of the islands and walked around naked—just me and the crabs. It was a fantastic feeling knowing I was the only person on the island.

Our next stops were Palm Island and Petite St. Vincent, very small and remote resort spots. On the way, we caught sight of a tiny island with one palm tree on it. We expected to see the lone survivor on it as so often depicted in cartoons.

On to Carriacou, where among the mangrove swamps, the men found oysters and came back with a bucket of them, much to Richard's delight. Grenada was our last port of call; St. George, the capital, was so picturesque. We went ashore walking up and down the hilly streets, buying trinkets and spices. After all, it is called Spice Island. It was sad to leave the *Ring Andersen*, its crew and the very knowledgeable captain and his friendly wife.

To get to the airport, we took two cabs that drove from one side of the island to the other, traveling on narrow roads that wound through tropical greenery until we reached 2,000 feet, where we had a breathtaking view of the coastline.

One of our favorite signs along the way was "Stop, sleeping policeman"—actually, bumps in the road to stops cars from speeding.

At the small airport, we boarded a LIAT plane. LIAT stood for Local Island Air Transport, but locally was known as Leave Island Any Time.

Since we had been virtually cut off from civilization, we heard no news—only a headline that said Nixon had resigned and Ford had been sworn in as the new president.

7. Chicago Happenings.

That same year, we had invited a few friends to our place to celebrate New Year's Eve. They included Rod and Vince and Peter Brown. We were having a discussion with Peter about the pros and cons of New York, where he lived, as opposed to Chicago. We said we thought crime was worse in New York. At that moment, we heard a loud cracking sound. A bullet had come through our third-floor living room window, making a hole in the drape and lodging into the wall opposite an inch from where Richard was standing. It just missed Vince's head as he sat low in a high-backed armchair. We immediately called 911 and, at 11:55 p.m. on New Year's Eve, two armed policemen came to our apartment. They said the same thing had happened to someone nearby and that, in all probability, it was some "nut" shooting to celebrate the New Year. So much for crime in New York!

We used to celebrate many holidays with Rod and Vince. They lived near us when we were on the South Side and moved to the North Side soon after we did. Nearly every Sunday we played poker and had dinner at whichever apartment we were in.

I always cooked Christmas dinner, and they and Birute usually joined us—for which occasion, I always made a traditional English Christmas pudding. I made it a couple of months ahead of time and fed a little extra brandy a few times before the day. Then I served it with brandy butter—a little rich but rather good.

Then for many years we shared a Fourth of July party—a little odd since Rod was Costa Rican, and Vince was Italian; we were English and, as such, shouldn't really be celebrating the day the Americans got rid of us. But those were good parties, which were usually progressive: cocktails and hors d'oeuvres in one home, then to the other for a buffet meal, and back to the first for dessert and more liquor. If the weather was hot, we would walk to Oak Street Beach (one of the great assets of the city) and swim to cool off.

On the subject of Oak Street Beach, while we were living on Dearborn Street, we often walked there. One summer day, while we were on our way to the beach, we noticed a young man with a lion cub on his shoulder walking in front of us. He went to the beach, too. The cub ran around and found a dog friend. They played together delightfully. Sometimes, the cub would run under someone's lounge chair and startle the occupant. The man and the cub spent a few weekends there, and the owner would carry the cub into the water. Many of us were enchanted by these antics until a few people objected. Thus, the man and his cub were not allowed to return. They lived near us. When we walked past their building, we were amused at the sign outside: "Beware the Lion." The cub was eventually given to a zoo.

Richard and I have often been asked why we chose to live in Chicago. First of all, we got our job offer and sponsorship in Chicago. Secondly, we had no money to go anywhere else for quite a few years. Thirdly, although we have never lived in New York, we have only been there for some weeks on end. We enjoy the quieter pace of Chicago, its many interests and its beauty, especially the wonders of Lake Michigan. We have never regretted our decision to stay here and have witnessed many changes in the city. When we arrived, the Prudential Building was one of the highest in the city, and there were street cars and trolley buses. While we were living on Dearborn, we saw the Hancock Building rise from ground level up from our back porch. One of the first expressways, the Edens, only went as far as Peterson Avenue. In the Loop, there were many theatres and movie houses; now, most of them are gone.

On our way to a movie house, while our studio was at 20 East Jackson, Richard and I bumped into my actor friend from the Gate Theatre in Dublin at the corner of State and Jackson. He was here with a touring company. What an amazing coincidence that we should meet in that spot among so many people.

That corner has special significance for us. When we visited Chicago with the Sadler's Wells Ballet in 1949, I took a photo of State Street from that same place. Little were we to know that, within five years, we would have ballet studios near that same intersection.

At State and Van Buren, a block away, stood a theatre that presented adult entertainment. One day, while we were at 20 East, we saw the name of the headliner on the marquee, Ineda Mann, which amused us. We were further amused when, a few days later, she arrived at our studio to sign up for classes. She was quite a good dancer and, after a few lessons, offered us tickets "to catch the show," which we did and were pleasantly surprised at her act.

It began with her sitting in a negligée at a boudoire, where she did some quite correct *developpés* while removing her shoes and hose. Then getting up, she continued her striptease act with some creditable ballet moves, like *grand jetés*.

A short while later, the theater was demolished. The wrecking company advertised the fact by putting up a sign that said, "We are the greatest strippers of them all."

8. Working With Ruth Page's Chicago Ballet.

During 1975, Ruth Page's Chicago Ballet was appearing at the Ruth Page Theatre at 1016 North Dearborn, an old Moose Lodge that also housed her school of dance. It was only two blocks away from our house.

Ruth had wanted Frederic Franklin to be her company director, but plans did not work out. Ben Stevenson came instead. Fred came though to produce some ballets for the company and, during that time, he stayed with us.

One day, walking up to Ruth's, Richard turned to Fred and said, "Who on earth would have thought that the two of us would be working for Ruth Page together?"

Richard and I were staging *One in Five* for her, and later we did *Façade*. They used our sets and costumes for both ballets. The reviews for *Façade* were excellent, comparing it most favorably with the Joffrey production. This time, Richard had complete control. Also, *Façade* was first performed on a similar small stage, the Mercury in London, and benefited from the intimate atmosphere.

9. Teaching With Robert Joffrey

At one of the parties we gave for Robert Joffrey and friends, Robert invited me to teach with him for a week in June at his Summer Workshop in Galveston, Texas. It was a wonderful opportunity but a hard decision to make since it would mean a lot of extra work for Richard during our busy summer term. But Richard was very supportive and said he could manage with help from a few former students. So I told Robert I would be honored to teach for him.

In Galveston, Robert, Richard Gibson and I were the only teachers the first week. I enjoyed watching Robert teach and being able to participate in the extracurricular activities, especially the dance films that were shown. Nearly every evening, Robert took a few of his staff to dinner, where there was always a vibrant exchange of ideas.

One evening he asked me to join him in Houston for a performance of *La Bayadere* by American Ballet Theatre. Rudolf Nureyev was the guest artist. Afterwards, Robert and I went to see Rudolf in his dressing room.

I agreed to be in Galveston one week only but, after learning that another teacher was unable to be there the second week, Robert asked me to stay. We called Richard, and he said he could manage all right. So I stayed the extra week and enjoyed the company of Diane Orio, one of the Joffrey company dancers, who also came to teach.

Richard began rehearsing for *The Nutcracker* again at the Arie Crown Theatre, and one of the rehearsals was being held at the Ruth Page studio. For his role as Herr Drosselmeyer, Richard had quite a few props, which included the "magic" cane that opened into a huge bunch of feather flowers, his voluminous cloak and a top hat. Since he needed all these things for the rehearsal, he asked permission to take the props with him.

Richard put everything into our car, which we parked on Washington Square (more commonly known as Bughouse Square) across the street from us. In the morning, when he went to collect the props on his way to Pages, to his utter horror he found they were gone. He felt terrible about the loss but was relieved when all the items were replaced. But, in retrospect, we laughed because at that time, Bughouse Square was a notorious gay hangout. We had visions of someone having a marvelous time parading around in Richard's cloak and top hat.

10. Ballet Russe de Monte Carlo Dancers.

In 1976, the Library and Museum of the Performing Arts in New York approached us with the purpose of adding an oral tape of our views and experiences to the archives. We agreed, and Nancy Reynolds—one of their representatives—came and interviewed us in Chicago. We also provided them with four videotapes of our Illinois Ballet performances on WTTW-Channel 11.

Our apartment on Dearborn Street seemed to be getting smaller and smaller. The longer we lived in Chicago, the more things we accumulated. It was time to find a larger place. We were sad to leave Dearborn Street, where we enjoyed some really good times—21 years in all. Some close and well-known friends had visited us, such as members of the Royal Ballet, including Margot Fonteyn, Robert Irving and Leslie Edwards.

When the Ballet Russe de Monte Carlo came to town, as they did once a year for a while, we saw quite a lot of the dancers, including Fred Franklin, Yvonne Chouteau, Miguel Terekov, Eugene Slavin, Gertrude Tyven, Perry Brunson and Meredith Baylis (a relative of Lilian Baylis'). They all came to visit us, and we always enjoyed their company.

These were the times when Alicia Alonso and Igor Youskevitch—a legendary partnership—were performing with Ballet Russe.

For a while we were so prejudiced in favor of Fonteyn that we that we didn't think anyone else could compare to her. But we came to greatly admire Alonso's wonderfully assured technique. Her partnership with Youskevitch, the epitome of a *premier danseur*, was delightful to watch, especially in Alonso's memorable performances as Giselle—all the more remarkable due to her near blindness.

We remember one time while waiting backstage for Fred at the Civic Opera House, Alonso came by for a drink at the water fountain and had trouble finding the fountain and the pedal. Meredith Baylis explained how she had to guide Alicia to the proper wings and help her on and off in the many entrances and exits she made in the second act of *Giselle*.

Chapter IX
1976-1980

1. Move to House on Mohawk Street. Franklin to Stay

We were now looking for a new apartment, and friends of Dick Carter's told us about a place on North Mohawk Street owned by a friend of theirs. It was a small clapboard house. The ground floor was occupied by an older lady; and the first and second floors were for rent as one unit. The owner, John Garrison, lived next door.

This was a big decision, especially as the rent was a little more than we were prepared to pay. Fred Franklin, who was staying with us at the time, helped us make our final decision to move to Mohawk Street, which we did in September.

We really liked the charming old house, which had a slight list to it. John Garrison installed a new floor in the living room to make it level. But when we hosted our first formal dinner in the dining room, we got the giggles after seeing that the wine in our glasses was not level. So we had to have a new floor put in there as well.

To get to the bedrooms on the top floor, we had to climb a very narrow, curved staircase. The furniture had to be hoisted up a ladder onto a small balcony and through double doors to our guest room. Such fun and games! The large kitchen had a small room off it, which became the cat's room.

Prior to that, we decided that G.T. might like to have a friend. We found an adorable kitten at the Anti-Cruelty Society, but asked them to keep her for us until our return from our annual holiday, which we spent in Hollywood, Florida.

When we returned, we picked up "Ellisa" (Ellis with an 'a'). She was black and white with asymmetrical markings, especially on her nose. We hoped she would be a nice companion for G.T.

But the first meeting of the two cats was disastrous. He snarled and spat at her. So we had to separate them. This happened every time he came near her.

G.T. had always slept at the foot of our bed. Now he came nowhere near us. He was obviously very upset with us for bringing an intruder into his home. Fred was staying with us, and the three of us were distraught over the situation. After a couple of days, we were seriously considering taking Ellisa back to the shelter.

Early the next morning, to my surprise, G.T. very slowly crept up our bed until he was level with my face, which he gave a little lick as if to say "I'm sorry." From then on, he and Ellisa became inseparable. Although they were both "fixed," they used to lie together kissing and licking and hugging each other. They were enchanting to watch.

After our move to Mohawk Street, Fred stayed with us for a week or more at a time while he was working for Ruth's company. We named our spare room "Fred's room."

It was a joy to have him around—his energy, sense of humor and boundless stories of his past experiences and exchanging stories of his and Richard's mutual friends. How I wish I had my tape recorder running on those many occasions.

Fred is also a marvelous cook. He usually finished his rehearsals long before we ended our teaching day. We would come home and smell the garlic cooking before we reached our front door. Then the "chef" would describe all the goodies we were about to partake of that particular evening. We were thoroughly spoilt, having a live-in master chef, and missed him sorely when he had to leave.

Soon after our move to Mohawk Street, we heard from a friend that Denis Rake had died. We still miss him so much—his genuine love for us, his sageness, his letters usually badly typed but always amusing. His delightful sense of humor got him through many trying times in his life.

Fred stayed with us five times from February to June, 1977. Ruth invited us to to stay at her place in St. Tropez again for our holiday. So after a short visit in England, we returned to Ruth's studio apartment. She had rented out the house to a French family.

During our various visits back to London, we tried to see some of our old friends. We nearly always saw Leslie Edwards who, with Richard, joined the Vic-Wells Ballet in 1933, and Moira Tucker, my roommate in the International Ballet. On occasion, we visited Wendy Toye who, one time arranged a party for some of the ex-members of the Markova-Dolin Ballet, which she had been in. Fred Franklin and Guy Massey were there. Wendy also intended it to be a surprise party for Robert (Bobby) Dorning, who had briefly shared a flat with Richard. Richard had not seen him for many years. The surprise worked, and Bobby was delightedly shocked. It was a great reunion. They all toasted Dolin and announced "Dancers for hire," as Dolin was directing the Festival Ballet at that time.

2. Audre Deckmann Mendel.

Audre Deckmann moved into Mohawk Street and cat sat for us while we were in Europe. She first came to us as a teenage student when we were at the Allegro School of Ballet. She was accompanied by her mother, a delicately beautiful woman. Audre, a beauty herself, was chosen as Miss Chicago one year. She also was a lovely dancer, with a special quality of lightness and grace. Audre joined the New York City Ballet for a brief time and Ballet Theatre, where she danced many roles.

After some bad injuries, she left Ballet Theatre and became the dance partner of Ed Sims with whom she performed for many years on stage and, as entertainment directors on the Norwegian Line cruise ships, they sailed around the world. They also performed at the St. Regis Roof in New York for a ten-week season to sold-out performances.

We happily met up with her again when she returned to Chicago. Audre and Ed were appearing at the Empire Room in the Palmer House, and we saw her too on her visits to see her parents, who lived near us. During one of these visits, she volunteered to cat sit for us. We have been close friends ever since. She is now Mrs. Herbert Mendel and living in Miami Beach, Florida, where we have spent many memorable times, as well as the house they had on a bluff by Lake Michigan in Benton Harbor. We enjoyed their wonderful hospitality and interesting guests. Sadly, Herb has passed away—a dear and generous man who had a genuine love of the arts.

On our return from Europe, we stopped in New York and spent a couple of nights with Fred Franklin and his friend Bill Ausman in their attractive penthouse with a large terrace that supports huge containers of tall trees and lovely plants—a treasure in the middle of bustling Manhattan. Our first meeting with Bill had been in Puerto Rico. We enjoyed him so much and on all the other times we've spent together.

Fred came to stay with us again in the fall. We were happy to have our "chef" back.

3. Richard Stages *Façade* for Houston Ballet. Royal Ballet.

Ben Stevenson, artistic director of Ruth Page's Chicago Ballet, was invited to be artistic director of the Houston Ballet. He accepted the position, where he stayed until his recent retirement. Soon after moving to Houston, he asked Richard to come down and stage *Façade* for the company. So Richard went to Houston early in 1978 and had the pleasure of not only working with the company dancers but also with Gwen Verdon, a friend of Ben's whom he had invited to dance the part of the Debutante with himself as the Gigolo—a rather hilarious duo.

Fred stayed with us on and off from February to June. He produced *Coppélia* Act II for Ruth's company, and Richard played the part of Dr. Coppélius, which he had done so well for Illinois Ballet. The only trouble he found was that, in Fred's production, everything that had been on the left was on the right, and vice versa.

The Royal Ballet performed at the Arie Crown Theatre in June, and we invited some of our company friends to a buffet dinner. Fred and his friend Bill were staying with us at the time. We also asked some of our Chicago friends to join us, including Ruth Page, who arrived with critic Clive Barnes in tow. Unaware that the Royal Ballet dancers were not too fond of Clive at that time, we were surprised and disappointed when almost at once they got up and left. Our other guests gradually said goodbye, leaving Fred, Bill and Clive Barnes, who stayed talking and talking with us. When he got up to leave, Clive asked Fred and Bill to share a cab with him. They rather smugly said they were staying with us.

On January 14th, 1979, Richard was at home having just had root canal; Audre was subbing for him at the studio. Winifred Haun who, after training with us, became a well-known modern dancer, was helping too. So we three were the last to leave the studio and found it was snowing heavily. The thought of getting a cab seemed hopeless, but Audre was able to hail one down. Fortunately, we were all going north. Audre got off first, and then we crawled up Lincoln Avenue. I was next, but the taxi driver refused to turn off to take me to Mohawk Street for fear of getting stuck in the snow. A bad winter, but it had improved a little when the Joffrey Ballet came in February. They nearly always came at that time of year and often had to contend with Chicago winters. In fact, their first appearance in the city was during a snow storm.

4. Port Grimaud.

Our holiday in 1979 started with a visit to my mother's home in Sussex for a week, during which time we went to see the Littleales—the English family we met in St. Tropez—in their beautiful house in Surrey. They were all packed and ready to drive with their car and boat to France. We arranged to meet them later at a rented house in Port Grimaud, near St. Tropez.

Port Grimaud is a man-made town, a sort of modern-day Venice, with charming houses, shops and restaurants accessible only by boats, which are moored outside the houses. We were able to take our car to the house, but only to leave our belongings. Then it had to be put in a huge parking lot until we left town.

We spent a fun week there. We sailed around in the Littleales' boat and enjoyed the delicious Grand Marnier crêpes, served through a window opening in a tiny shop. Also in Port Grimaud, we had the best pizzas ever, made of puff pastry. Ah! The simple pleasures of life!

On our way back to Chicago, we spent one night in Nice (the time we went on our disappointing search for the villa on Cap Ferrat).

Soon after our return, our dear friend Vince died of cancer. We knew he was ill, but it was nonetheless a shock and a great loss. We saw Rod a few times after our move to Wells Street; then he stopped coming. Some years later, we heard from a mutual friend that he was selling all the lovely things in his apartment. Then Rod just disappeared. We have the feeling he went home to Costa Rico. How strange life and relationships are.

Another unfortunate incident occurred this year. We had rented our *Façade* costumes to the Maryland Ballet. They had a fire and lost a lot of costumes, including our *Façade* ones. Gordon Schmidt, a former student who was in the Maryland Ballet at the time, informed us that only one straw boater from the "Popular Song" dance was left. Besides being upsetting, we received no compensation for the destroyed costumes.

We had more bad news. John Garrison, our landlord, was an alcoholic. He would drink at least one large bottle of liquor a day. He literally drank himself to death. This was late in the year, and we heard that the house was going to be put on the market. We were once again having to search for a new home.

Chapter X
1980-1987

1. Condo on Wells Street. Meeting Stanley Paul.

We decided it was time to find a condo, not a rental. So in early 1980, we began our search. But we were picky, hoping for a place with high ceilings, a fireplace and at least a balcony or porch. We must have looked at 20 or more apartments, none of which appealed to us. Then a real estate agent told us that a friend of hers wanted to sell one floor of the house he had recently bought. When she told us it was on Wells Street in Old Town, we were a little taken aback. For some years Wells Street had a bad reputation, but it was improving. We agreed to see the apartment and, as the agent said, it had everything we were looking for. As soon as we walked into the building, we had a good feeling.

Despite being piled high with packing cases, we were able to see that there were high ceilings and a fireplace in the living room, which also had ceiling-to-floor windows. The fireplace surround and the baseboards were made of marble and tile, and there was a large terrace. We had to wait a week before meeting the owner, Stanley Paul, the well-known society orchestra leader. When we met, we got on so well, having quite a few mutual friends.

Stanley was living in what would be our apartment, while the top two floors were being converted for himself. We were able to move in at the beginning of June. As with all our homes, we designed the lay out and decorated them ourselves. The idea of someone else doing something so personal never appealed to us.

When we first arrived in Chicago to live, we had only a couple of suitcases and one steamer trunk. Over the years we have collected, been given or bequeathed various objects and books—all of which have helped to make our homes individual. Richard, an excellent non-professional carpenter, made our shelving and bookcases. I've always made our drapes and curtains, except when we moved to Mohawk and Wells streets. At that time, Paul Parenteau, the owner of the Parenteau Studios where some of the best indoor furnishings were made, generously made drapes, covers and blinds for us. We first met Paul when his talented daughter, Ilya, came to study with us.

We have always been fairly frugal. At times, we've roamed our nearby alleys and found some lasting items in good condition—cabinets, mirrors, wicker chairs, a barbeque pit, among other things. Another "find," one of our favorite possessions, is a large framed reproduction of the Leon Bakst design for Vaslav Nijinsky in *The Afternoon of a Faun*. There is a story behind our acquiring it. While we were living on Dearborn Street, we usually took a bus to the studio and passed an art shop at the corner of State and Kinzie streets. One day I saw the Bakst in the window, with other art works, on sale for $10 each. I told Richard about it, and we decided that, even though $10 was a lot of money for us then, we had to buy it. The next day, we rushed off the bus and were happy to see it was still there. When we entered the shop, we asked the young woman behind the counter, "How much is the Bakst in the window?" She looked blankly at us and said, "Ugh," as though we were asking "How much is the doggie in the window?"

She got it out, and we paid the $10. Then we left as fast as we could. On close inspection at home, we found it was really special. The frame alone was worth much more than $10. We have been told that our print is one of three made from the original, which was once owned by Rebekah Harkness.

One of the first guests to stay in our new home was my "stepmother" Jane. As a representative of the city of Dover, Kent, she was on a goodwill tour to some of the American towns named Dover. It was wonderful to see her. She was always so witty, sage and full of life. Incidentally, one of Jane's best friends, an old school mate, was Janet Auchincloss, Jacqueline Kennedy's mother. We met her and her husband, Hugh D., at a party given by my father and Jane when they were living on Pont Street in London. In an enchanting book that Jacqueline and her sister Lee wrote about their first trip together to Europe, they mention Mrs. Du Boulay and that, in a telegram, Mrs. Du Boulay had invited them to cocktails. Beside this section in our copy of their book, Jane wrote, "and we had fun too!—Du Boulay." Years later, we met Lee at a party Ruth Page was giving for Nureyev.

Fred also came to stay shortly after.

For some years after our car was badly damaged while parked outside a friend's house while we were celebrating New Year's Eve, we swore never to go out again on that occasion. We celebrated at home instead, thus starting a tradition of inviting friends to our place. In 1980, we threw one of the biggest parties, partly because we had such a large living room and also because Richard enjoyed asking some of the dancers from *The Nutcracker*.

During this year, our friends Ted and Barbara Wilson were planning to start a small ballet company. They were not dancers but had many influential friends and associates. They arranged for John Prinz, a principal dancer with American Ballet Theatre, to come as company director. John had been a student of ours for some years when he was a boy.

We had known the Wilsons for a while after first seeing them at many of the same performances and wondering who the attractive couple was. One day we were all invited to a mutual friend's place. Ted and Barbara knew who we were and had been wanting to meet us. We hit it off and became close friends.

Ted and Barbara asked us for permission to use the name Illinois Ballet. They hoped to call the company Illinois Ballet Theatre, which was alright with us. They arranged for a "calling card" performance, which included Audre Deckmann and Ed Sims. All went well until one of the promised backers announced that Maria Tallchief was starting a company and felt it would not be a good idea to compete with her. It was a disastrous statement, causing the whole idea to fall flat, and the Illinois Ballet Theatre never left the ground.

As far as we were concerned, one good thing came out of that event. We got to know Larry Selander better after talking to him at the reception following the program. We first met Larry at Sylvia Black's. She and her husband Ben had not only helped us open our own ballet school, but Ben being a lawyer, always helped with any legal problems. After his untimely death, we asked Sylvia if she knew of anyone who could help us in the future. She introduced us to Larry, who was the son of a friend of hers. We liked him immediately and got on very well.

The first of many kindnesses Larry did for us was help us make decisions about leaving Mohawk Street after John Garrison's death, and working with Stanley Paul and his lawyer about buying the condo at 1511 N. Wells Street. We cherish our friendship with Larry and his wife Mary. They, and his mother Esther, have made us feel like family members.

In May of that year, I went to Ann Arbor, Michigan to stage *Aurora's Wedding* for the Ann Arbor Civic Ballet, a small company directed by Sylvia Hamer, a dear lady and well-respected teacher in Michigan. For some years prior to this, I had gone to Ann Arbor at Sylvia's request to teach at her school and stage *Giselle* Act II and other dances for her company. *Aurora's Wedding* was to be her farewell program after announcing her retirement. Birute Barodicaite came with me and danced the role of Aurora at the performance.

Over the years, Richard and I have taught at many dance schools and conventions. We went many times to Butler University Dance Department; we both have taught at the Chicago National Association of Dance—although we were off their list for a while after we voiced our opinions about "pointe," or as they like to say, "toe" work.

I have taught in Flint, Grand Rapids, Ann Arbor and Detroit, Michigan; Springfield, Illinois; and Spokane, Washington, as well as the aforementioned time in Galveston with Robert Joffrey.

During a dance convention being held in a hotel ballroom, the crowded room became very noisy. Even with a microphone, I found it hard to be heard. So I turned to someone nearby and said, "Oh for a whistle." A few moments later, she produced one which I happily used and was able to get a little more law and order.

2. Joffrey Ballet Center Concert Dancers. Another Studio Move.

In 1981, I received an invitation from Edith D'Addario, director of the Joffrey School of Ballet in New York, to stage works for the Joffrey Ballet Center Concert Dancers for their appearance at the Grand Rapids, Michigan Summerfest in August. I set the first two movements of *Valse Promenade* and the *Peasant Pas de Deux* from *Giselle* Act I. We used the costumes from the Illinois Ballet wardrobe. I rehearsed for about four days in Grand Rapids, starting the day by teaching company class. The dancers were a pleasure to work with. *Valse* and *Peasant* were part of an overall program that consisted of four other ballets.

During that year we made yet another studio change—seems we had the seven-year itch. Changes were being made at 17 N. State, which did not suit us. So we went looking for new space, not easy as so many buildings had low ceilings.

We finally found space on the top floor of 185 N. Wabash Avenue, a vacated series of offices, which offered potential without too many alterations. We had to lay the obligatory new floor—such a fuss over dance floors these days. We look back at all the floors and stages we danced on. The Metropolitan Opera House in New York, with all its "potholes" one had to maneuver around, immediately comes to mind. We suffered no more injuries, maybe less, than dancers have today with all the special floors that need to be laid for them in studios and on stages.

In January 1982, the *Chicago Tribune* published a very nice article about us in the Sunday "Parade" section. In fact, we had a lot of good publicity this year. We had another article about Richard and me in the *Tribune* and one in the *Sun-Times*. On the subject of publicity, we had some good television interviews. Once, when Richard was in *The Nutcracker*, he was interviewed by Harry Porterfield on the program, "Someone You Should Know." Another time, we were both interviewed in the studio and at home for a local ABC program.

That year, we also had a visit from our dear friend Ray Powell, who gave us his ballet, *One in Five*, in the early days of Illinois Ballet. He was on his way back to Australia after seeing friends in England.

When Ray did leave the Sadler's Wells Ballet, he moved to Melbourne, Australia. Peggy Van Praagh, who started the Australian Ballet, invited him to come as ballet master—a position he held for many years. He appeared in various roles in the company. Even in retirement, he still made cameo appearances.

3. My Mother.

Early in 1983, I received disturbing news from England that my mother was not well and had been hospitalized. I had to go and see what was wrong. It was February, and after making plans for someone to help Richard at the school, I left for Garden Cottage. Friends me me at the local station after my train trip from London.

At Garden Cottage, I found a letter from my mother explaining her condition. She had been so upset about having to put Hil into a home that she neglected her own health. She became dehydrated and weak. Fortunately friends had called her doctor, and he insisted on her going to hospital immediately.

I arranged for a rental car and drove to the hospital in Eastbourne the next day (my first time driving on the left) and saw my mother who was much better. I was able to take her home the next day. Friends had already set up a bed in the living room so she didn't have to walk upstairs to her bedroom.

It was obvious that my mother would be best off in a home, especially the wonderful one nearby, named Weald House, that Hil was in already. I got her to agree to go there temporarily after finding out they had a lovely room vacant in a week's time. But it took a week of diplomacy on my part to persuade my naturally reluctant mother that it would be best for her to stay there permanently. As soon as she agreed, we made arrangements for Garden Cottage to be put on the market. I immediately started to itemize belongings, furniture, etc. I ran up and down stairs all day asking my mother what she wanted done with this or that, cleaning out drawers and cupboards. One drawer was full of letters from me. I sorted through them, keeping ones that referred to our travels. These have been very helpful in refreshing my memory for this book.

The attic was full of forgotten treasures and memories. It was hard to be drastic and discard some beloved items. My darling mother wanted me to have so much, but it was not practical to bring too many things back with me. I already had a case full. My mother also had to decide on the few things she would have room for in her new home. I got a lot done before I had to leave. A close friend was going to continue the job of clearing up and organizing an auction.

On my last day, I drove my mother to Weald House and helped her settle in. She was happy to be near Hil again, though I am afraid dear Hil sadly knew little of what was happening. I was just so grateful to know that I was leaving them in very good care. The man and his wife who ran the home were the finest people. But it was with a heavy heart that I said goodbye to my mother and Hil. It was to be the last time I saw them.

Richard continued his role of Herr Drosselmeyer, and 1984 marked his 15th year. He was enjoying it more and more, as once he really knew the role, he was able to add touches of his own. Richard loved portraying the older characters, such as Herr Drosselmeyer and Dr. Coppélius. He wishes more classical dancers would make the transition from virtuoso to character roles. Some dancers seem to feel it is demeaning. But that is not so. They can add such depth to ballets requiring older characters. In *The Nutcracker*, Richard enjoyed the annual meeting of the many good dancers who were chosen for the lead roles, and working with the young Claras and Nutcracker Princes, many of whom went on to dance in major companies.

4. Edna McRae.

Larry Selander approached us with a proposal. He wanted to help the school obtain not-for-profit status in order for it to receive some monetary support. Larry and a group of friends got together and put the plan into action, with our blessing and gratitude. Most of them also agreed to be on our board, which was deemed a necessity. We also decided to create an advisory board, and were fortunate to have some well-known people agree to this position. Dame Margot Fonteyn said she would be delighted in a letter written from Panama. Robert Joffrey, Gerald Arpino, Freddie Franklin, Audre Deckmann Mendel, Edna McRae and an ex-student of hers, Marilyn Miglin, were on our board. It was proposed that we make the school's new status known publicly by holding a fundraiser, combined with a reception honoring Edna McRae, the well-known retired dance teacher.

We heard of Edna McRae as soon as we arrived in Chicago. We felt then that none of the established ballet teachers were too pleased to have us in town. They were probably even more unhappy when some of their students came to study with us. So the atmosphere for many years remained rather cool, compounded a little by our ingrained English reserve. Hence, there was little or no communication between us.

Our friend P.W. Manchester had encouraged us to get together with Edna. We finally did. It was a pleasure, and we got on well. Edna asked me to help her with a program for an event in Evanston, which involved a couple of our dancers. She was most kind and appreciative of the outcome.

Richard used to work with her during the days when she was in charge of the children appearing in *The Nutcracker*, since the role of Herr Drosselmeyer required a lot of rehearsing with the children in the party scene, as well as with Clara and the Nutcracker Prince later.

Richard and I arranged to meet with her and tell her of our hopes: 1) that she would allow us to start a scholarship program in her name, 2) that she would agree to be on our advisory board, and 3) let us have the reception for her. She was delighted with everything and willing to let us use her name in any way we saw fit.

The board then set to work finalizing plans for the reception. It would be held on Sunday, October 27th, 1985 at the historic Cliff Dwellers Club on Michigan Avenue. Richard and I were responsible for the short dance program. We decided on a little class demonstration to be followed by an excerpt from *Pas de Quatre*, and for Lori Romito, an ex-student of ours who was dancing with the Milwaukee Ballet, and Gordon Schmidt to perform the opening movement of the *Don Quixote* "Pas de Deux".

The board also produced a beautiful brochure to be presented to all the invitees. It included a short history of Richard and me and the school, photos of us, a list of professional dancers who had been trained by us, and more.

5. My Mother. Airplane Problems.

There was much to be done, and all was going well until October 14th when I received the awful news that my darling mother had passed away in her sleep. She was 84. I was devastated and felt a dreadful guilt because I had not been to see her again after leaving her at Weald House. But our visits had always been about two years apart. Then there was the dilemma about going to England. I spoke to my Aunt Alison, always my closest, and explained to her the importance of the upcoming reception as far as the school was concerned. She said that I must stay and see it through and that my mother would not have wished for me to miss such an important occasion. She also told me that my mother had always been so proud of our work. Alison said to come as soon as the reception was over. Albeit reluctantly, I took her advice and stayed.

The reception was a success, thanks to all the help we had and the excellent turnout. An added pleasure was that our dear friend and neighbor, Stanley Paul, offered to play for us at the reception. Many of Edna's ex-students attended, which delighted her.

I left for England the day after the reception. Thanks to the kindness of the couple who owned and ran Weald House, I was given a room there.

My mother had been cremated the week before, so I went to collect her ashes. Because she left no instructions for their disposal, I took it upon myself to carry them to the Downs near Alfriston, Sussex, where she told me she had taken Hil's ashes. Hil had died just two months earlier. In my rented car, I made the pilgrimage to Alfriston and, there, scattered her ashes into the wind over the beautiful Downs where she and Hil, Richard and I had enjoyed many happy picnics.

With much help from the priest at the church she attended, we arranged for a small memorial service. Many people attended, most of them strangers to me, but they were so kind and full of words of praise for my mother.

I did indeed have a wonderful mother. Without complaint, she reared me all alone from the time I was six through many lean years. When I thought I wanted to be a ballet dancer, she never objected but let me make up my own mind. When I was certain that was what I wanted, she gave me help and encouragement.

When Richard and I told her of our decision to accept the teaching position in Chicago, I believe it must have hurt, knowing that her only child would be living so far away. This was my only regret about living in Chicago, especially as she got older. But, as always, she wanted only what was best for us and gave us her blessing in her usual unselfish way. She was one of the kindest and most caring people ever. Being Irish, she had what we call "the gift of the gab," never at a loss for words. This made her a wonderful correspondent; she wrote to us almost every week.

She did make two visits to see us in Chicago, but long before we had our house in Michigan. How I wish that she could have seen it and our garden. I wish, too, that she would know that I am painting again. But I have a feeling she knows all this and is happy for us.

In her later years, she became quite religious, and I am grateful that her faith sustained her to the end.

Now both my parents are gone, and Richard feels the loss, too, as my family was the only one he ever really felt a part of. He adored my mother; it was a mutual affection.

At Weald House, I tackled the job of clearing up her belongings. She had left everything to me. I arranged for a few items to be shipped to Chicago; a few I gave to Weald House and the staff; and some to the local Goodwill.

I also found a handwritten journal compiled by my mother's great-uncle who had lived at Sally Park. It traced the history of the Handcock family and various members, dating back to about 1600. I brought it back with me and had a a most interesting time copying it. The handwriting was beautiful, but I did have trouble deciphering parts of it.

When all was done, I left Weald House and drove to Sandwich to see Jane. From there, I spent one night with the Littleales, who drove me to London the next day where I spent one night with Michael Jervis and Ann Morley. They then drove me to Heathrow, where I had to wait eight hours because of a baggage handlers' strike. Somehow I managed to secure a seat by a window in the lounge, and there I stayed. A good spot! A kind person held it for me while I went in search of a sandwich, which I brought back and downed with a much-needed drink.

I seemed fated to have problems with my flights to Chicago. Two years before, on returning from seeing my mother and bringing back a suitcase of treasures, all went well until just before we landed at Chicago's O'Hare Airport. That's when the captain announced he had been informed that there was possibly a bomb on board! He told us to keep calm and that all was being done to get us down safely. We were to land at a remote part of the airport, where buses would take us away from the plane and to the terminal. Everyone behaved very well, and we did land safely. We got off with no panic, and the buses were waiting for us. But it seemed forever before they drove off, leaving us to think that the plane would blow up right beside us.

We got to the terminal, where we waited three hours while they checked all the luggage. Meanwhile, Richard was waiting in the reception area. Upon inquiring about the delay, he was informed by a TV crew that the plane had a bomb on it—poor Richard. When we finally got our luggage, the customs agents said because it was so late and everyone had waited so long, we could all leave. During all this time, I kept thinking that the lovely things I had brought back from England might all be blown up.

6. Scholarship Auditions. Joffrey TV Program.

On January 26th, 1986, we held the first auditions for the scholarship to be offered to two dancers with money from the Edna McRae Scholarship Fund. Edna herself agreed to be a judge, as did Robert Joffrey, Brunilda Ruiz and Basil Thompson—quite an impressive panel. There was a good turnout, no pun intended. Two talented dancers were chosen by unanimous decisions. Afterwards the judges, Brunilda's husband, Paul Sutherland, and a few other friends came back to our apartment for a little buffet gathering.

There was a time when Paul and I were teaching at the same dance convention. It was his first time, and he had made copious class notes. He showed them to me and asked if I thought there were too many. I told him that, quite honestly, I didn't think he would need so much, good as they were. Afterwards, he told me I was right. On seeing the caliber of the class, he didn't use any of his notes.

During the year, we realized that our dear cat Ellisa was obviously not well. We kept finding lumps on her body. The vet told us the bad news that she had skin cancer and that treatment would be the same as for humans—chemotherapy. We sadly made the dreadful decision to have her put to sleep. The vet did not press us, but later said we had made the right choice. She had been such a delightful character and a joy to us.

We missed her so much, as did G.T. He lost hair from his stomach, evidently a sign of stress. He regained the hair but was obviously lonely.

During our summer break, we flew to Denver to visit friends who had a house in Georgetown. We stayed a couple of days enjoying the wonderful trips we were taken on, once near the Continental Divide. The scenery was spectacular, and the weather was perfect.

From Denver, we went to Reno to see my cousin Jillian and Mitch and their little daughter Michelle. They drove us to beautiful Lake Tahoe.

Then on to San Francisco for two nights, our first visit there since the Sadler's Wells Ballet tour. We rented a car for the rest of our trip.

We continued on to San Jose to stay one night with Terry Anzur's parents before we set off on our long drive to Santa Barbara. Terry had been a TV reporter and anchorwoman on CBS News in Chicago for a few years and had come to us for ballet classes. She was a good dancer, and we enjoyed having her in class and as a friend.

After leaving San Jose, we stopped for a night in Monterey, went to Carmel, and then on the crazy but magnificent drive along Big Sur.

While in Santa Barbara for two days, we contacted Catherine (Katie) Boulton, who was on the Sadler's Wells Ballet's second American tour. When we were in New York, she went out on a blind date and met Brooks Firestone (of the Firestone Tire family). They later married and were living near Santa Barbara, where they owned and operated the Firestone vineyards. Sadly, Katie was indisposed; so we were only able to meet by phone.

Then we went on to our final destination, La Jolla, another delightful spot. We also enjoyed visiting nearby San Diego.

On October 26th, we held a second scholarship audition and again Basil came down from Milwaukee Ballet to be an adjudicator. Pamela Johnson, who had left the Joffrey Ballet company to get married and return to the Chicago area, was also a judge.

The Joffrey Ballet was in town again in March 1987 and, as always, Robert invited us to any performance at the Auditorium Theatre we were able to attend. We went to at least five programs and, for most, we sat in the staff box with Robert.

On the Sunday of their visit, the Joffrey School held its Chicago audition in our studio. In the evening we gave a party, with of course trifle for Robert. Another time when the Joffrey Ballet came to town, Robert was invited by WGN-TV to do a program about ballet. He decided to do one explaining briefly the progression of a dancer from beginning to professional. We were delighted when he asked if he could use three of our young students to demonstrate the first part, and then he used company dancers. Our students were thrilled. Robert gave them a short rehearsal as to what they were to do, which was mostly at the barre. They really performed well, and Robert was very pleased with them, as were we.

7. First Choreographic Effort. Ted and Barbara Wilson. Visit to Europe.

Giving thought to our annual student class demonstration, I decided to try my hand at choreography—something neither of us had ever done. Because we already had the attractive costumes from *Con Gioco*, a ballet that George Montaigne had done for Illinois Ballet, I thought I would use them and some of the same Dohnanyi score. The students seemed to enjoy what I was doing, and I was delighted at how well they performed.

For the Memorial Day weekend, we stayed with our close friends Ted and Barbara Wilson. They had bought a charming house in a secluded spot in Sawyer, Michigan, about an hour-and-a- half drive from Chicago. We visited them quite a few times previously and always had such a good time. Ted was an excellent cook. But on this occasion, we were distressed to see Barbara looking very thin and tired. She assured us it was just because she had been working so hard. We were with them again for the Fourth of July. This time, Barbara was visibly not well and spent much of the time in bed. Again, she said she just needed a holiday, which they were planning for early August. They were going to England to stay with Anthony Dowell, the famous dancer, and presently director of the Royal Ballet. The Wilsons and Anthony had become good friends during his time in America.

As it happened, we were planning to go to England in August. So we discussed getting together at some point. But just before we left, we received a call from a mutual friend telling us that Barbara had died of cancer in an English hospital. It was shocking and dreadful news. We were deeply saddened at the loss of a dear friend, all the more so since she and Ted were away from home.

We were able to contact Ted at Anthony's house in London. He was still in shock but begged us to come and see him when we got to London.

We went through with our plans to stay with friends in Surrey, visit my aunts in Winchester, and stay with Jane in Sandwich before reaching London. When we did, Anthony kindly invited us to lunch at his beautiful house by the River Thames. Despite our sadness, it was a nice occasion, and Ted seemed to be coping well and happy to see us—his first contact with friends from home.

From England, we sailed by Hovercraft to Boulogne, and then to Paris, where we boarded one of those fabulous French trains. The glass of water on the table never wobbled, even at 120 m.p.h.

We got off at Lyon, picked up a car and drove to Geneva, Switzerland, where we had lunch and one of the best cheese omelets ever. From there, we drove around the lake to Montreaux and spent the night there, giving us time to walk around and savor the fabulous scenery.

Returning to Geneva, we followed our mapped route into France and south through Annecy, Grenoble and on to Aix-en-Provence, where we stayed the night.

We were aiming for St. Tropez again but had made no reservations. There was no Herbe Folle to go to, since Ruth had decided to sell it.

Arriving in St. Tropez early in the morning, we went searching for lodgings and, fairly soon, saw a sign up a little cul-de-sac near the Place des Lices. The pension looked nice, and we were told if we returned in one hour we could have a room. We were indeed in luck, for the place was run by a delightful family. We had a clean room with a lovely view and a courtyard, where we enjoyed our coffee and croissants every morning for the ten days we were there.

Most days we spent at the nude beach and enjoyed excellent food there at lunchtime. We usually ate dinner in town. We went to the market at the Place des Lices, saw a local circus and visited the art museum. Then it was back to reality, a new school year and another season of *The Nutcracker* for Richard.

I decided to try choreographing again and worked on a short piece to Edward Elgar's music, with the thought of using five girls and one boy in the costumes from *Memento*. The theme was about young people meeting and having a good time. I called it *Les Jeunes Amis*. We also planned to repeat our version of *Les Sylphides*, with the three lead girls and the boy. There were some very talented students in the Advanced Class at that time, a pleasure to work with. Rehearsals started in early March.

Herbe Folle in St. Tropez.

This Persistent Image on WTTW TV. Peggy Powell, Richard, myself, Dom Orejudos.

Myself with Ruth Page in our studio.

With Frederic Franklin on his terrace in New York.

Robert Joffrey, Richard, Edna McRae, Brunilda Ruiz, myself, Basil Thompson in our studio.

HRH Queen Elizabeth, Julia Farron, Richard. Photo: Keith Saunders.

HRH Queen Elizabeth, Leslie Edwards, Margaret Dale, Pauline Clayden, myself.
Photo: Keith Saunders.

Chapter XI
1987-1993

1. Painting Again. Robert Joffrey. Frederick Ashton.

Ted was alone, so we tried to see him as often as possible. One day he was having dinner with us, and the subject of painting came up. He had studied painting in college, and I told him of my studies. He asked if I had any of my works to show him. I had kept a few things, which I showed him. He thought they were good and encouraged me to start again.

After he left, I felt inspired to get out my painting equipment, which went back to my school days. There was a time, after I left school, when I wondered about my future—whether to be an artist or a ballet dancer. I thought I can paint later in life, even if in a wheelchair. But ballet is a short-lived profession and for the young, making my decision fairly easy. So happily, not in a wheelchair, my lifestyle had changed and the thought of returning to painting appealed to me. Amazingly, some of the tubes of watercolor were still usable. I did a small painting and was happy that I hadn't forgotten everything. I continued to do more, all landscapes, and got further encouragement from Richard and Ted. One day Ted brought a friend with him, and the friend bought one of my paintings—my first sale.

The school demonstration class was held at the Ruth Page Foundation Auditorium and was very successful. The students did well, and we received high praise.

For a time, we had been hearing depressing rumors that Robert Joffrey was ill. But that did not help to steel us when we heard of his death in 1988. What a terrible loss to the ballet world; how tragic for the company that he and Gerald Arpino created. We, too, had lost a good friend.

Robert and Gerry built their original small group of dancers into an internationally respected company. Robert had always been determined to preserve some of the older prominent ballets by early 20th century choreographers. He achieved this, allowing newer generations to see the works of Massine, Michel Fokine, Nijinsky and Ashton that are seldom, if ever, seen elsewhere. They continue to be produced with such love and care.

This was to be a tragic year for the ballet world. We lost not only Robert Joffrey but also Sir Frederick Ashton. Dear Sir Fred, what marvelous memories we have of him personally and of all the treasures he created. We hope the Royal Ballet and others, such as the Joffrey Ballet, always keep his works in their repertoires.

I champion ballet companies that keep the classics in their repertoire, especially when they adhere as closely as possible to the original concept. These are part of our heritage and must never be lost. Unfortunately, not many ballets are notated. It is a complicated and difficult system. Not many people can read the few systems that exist, unlike musical scores which so many can read and perform from. Nowadays, at least, there are videos of many of the great ballets, though not with the original casts. They are, therefore, interpretations. But, nonetheless, it is a way of preserving great works—for that we must be grateful.

2. Johan Renvall. Filming *Desire*.

The Fourth of July weekend, Richard and I went to Michigan to stay with Ted. American Ballet Theatre dancers Craig Wright and Johan Renvall also were staying with him. Johan told us he would be starring in a film called *Desire*, which was to be filmed in Chicago. The story dealt with the preparations for a dance school graduation performance, with all the accompanying trauma, bickering, competitiveness and love problems.

The director was still looking to fill the role of Johan's mother. Johan thought I would be perfect as the mother, since she was an ex-dancer. He arranged for me to meet the director. I was given the part and the lines I would have to speak, which I religiously tried to learn.

On the day of shooting, I was in a scene filmed outside a house on Sedgwick Street. They changed some of my lines and cut others, which meant I might as well not bothered to learn any lines in the first place. Show business! Nevertheless, the scene went fairly well, except for two incidents. First, we had to wait for a garbage truck to move and secondly, without anyone's knowledge, the owners of the next-door house were having their walkway newly cemented. So everything was held up until that was completed. And then, after resuming work, we heard a shout from someone in the crew: a squirrel had just fallen into the wet cement!

Then more trauma followed. The studio and stage sections of the film were shot at Niles High School Auditorium. I was told that someone would telephone me and let me know when I was needed for my brief appearance as Johan's mother sitting in the audience at the graduation performance. But I received no call—that is, not until 7 o'clock one morning when someone on the staff telephoned me saying they had forgotten to call me and could I be in Niles by 8 o'clock. I leapt out of bed and found some clothes suitable for being at a performance—forgot earrings—and dashed out. I drove all the way to Niles and lost my way trying to find the school. When I finally arrived, Craig rushed me to the make-up room and then I was rushed to my seat in the auditorium. One of the staff stood on the stage and apologized for the delay, saying they had forgotten to inform me of the filming time, added to which they had hired extras to be the audience. The extras had been sitting there for over an hour. When the film came out, I was only shown in that scene for one fleeting moment.

Meanwhile, Ted and an associate had opened an antique shop in Sawyer, Michigan, and kindly offered to display some of my paintings. At the same time, I was exhibiting a few of them in an art shop on Wells Street.

3. First Watercolor Exhibit. House in Michigan. Italy and France.

On May 7th, 1989, I had my first watercolor exhibition. It was held in our ballet studio. Richard suggested covering the mirrors with black cloth, which worked well. I hung about three or four paintings with picture hooks on each mirror and some on the walls.

Because we were using the studio for classes on Saturday, we had to wait until everyone left to set up. With the help of one of our students, Kathy Kerstowske, we got everything ready for the opening on Sunday. All went well, and I sold several paintings.

Over the course of our visits to Ted, we made some nice acquaintances who often urged us to buy a house of our own. At first it seemed impractical because we were teaching until 5 or 6 o'clock at night on Saturdays. That left us only one day free. But circumstances started to change. I gave up teaching the children's classes, cutting down the hours on Saturdays. After some time, we seriously started looking for a house.

Ted's antique shop was on Tower Hill Road in Sawyer. One day his partner said he knew of a house about to be put on the market. It was also on Tower Hill Road, a short walk from the shop. We arranged to see it and liked it straight away. It was the right size and an ideal location. We saw its potential despite the fact that there was a wall dividing the main room into two. We decided to buy the house.

Some years earlier, we had stopped on the expressway near Sawyer. I was teaching in Grand Rapids, and Richard came to take me home by car. It was not a good trip back to Chicago. First, the generator went out—a bad situation on a dark night. We were nearing the town of Holland and had to spend the night in a motel while the generator was being fixed. We started on our way again when suddenly the radiator burst and water began shooting all over the place. Fortunately, we were near a truck stop in Sawyer and managed to get help. But the mechanic said he would have to go to New Buffalo for new parts. We thought New Buffalo, where on earth is that?

We were growing worried about time. I was supposed to be back at the studio on Michigan Avenue to teach a noon class. We called Dom and asked him to start class if I was late. Eventually the radiator was fixed, and we were on our way to Chicago with time running short. Richard dropped me off in front of the Fine Arts Building, and I entered the studio just as Dom was finishing *pliés*. Whew! Anyhow, we now know exactly where Sawyer and New Buffalo are.

As it happened, before we bought the house, we already arranged for a trip to Europe and prayed we had enough money.

We flew to Paris in early August and had lunch with Bruce Merrill, who was teaching ballet in Paris. From Paris, we took a train for an overnight journey to Florence. There we picked up a rented car and then found our hotel. For three wonderful days, we re-explored Florence, that most beautiful city. We went, among other sites, to the Pitti Palace and Boboli Gardens and spent one day going to Fiesole, which we had visited years before when we were on tour with the Sadler's Wells Ballet.

From Florence, we drove to Viareggio on the west coast and north along the coast much of the way, when not driving through the countless tunnels built into the mountains. We had lunch in Lirice, which intrigued us because we had an old print of the area at home.

Our next stop was Santa Margherita, where we were booked into a lovely hotel. The next day we took the ferry to that heavenly place called Portofino. The entire Italian Riviera was so beautiful, especially as we were blessed with good weather.

We spent the day in Portofino and got the ferry back to Santa Margherita for one more night. From there we drove to Genoa, where we had lunch. We continued on to San Remo for one night, then drove through Monte Carlo to Eze, where we stopped for a late breakfast. After leaving Eze, we made a wrong turn and found ourselves in a precarious position. The terrain is very high with precipitous drops. The car had a slipping clutch, which Richard had maneuvered very well so far. But if he had not been able to control it while reversing on this occasion, we would have plunged over the edge of the cliff! Luckily, all was went and we were safely on our way to St. Tropez, where we had made reservations at the charming pension we stayed at before.

Each time we went to St. Tropez, we savored the wonderful French cuisine. Even at the beach, which we visited almost daily, the food was excellent. Richard enjoyed the large *moules* (mussels), and I the fresh and enticing salads. A few times for our evening meal, we drove to nearby villages. We loved dining in Gassin and Ramatuelle—so picturesque. We accompanied nearly all our meals with a bottle or carafe of the local *vin rosé*—my mouth waters at the thought.

We flew back to Chicago from Nice, where we spent our last day. That evening while driving to Villefranche, we saw what looked like an attractive restaurant. We got a table outside near the water. It was a glorious moonlit night, with the path of the moon shimmering across the bay toward Cap Ferrat and its twinkling lights—a most romantic and memorable night.

Soon after our return to Chicago, we closed on the house but had to wait until early October to get the key.

The first thing we did was find out if the wall in the main room could be taken down without too much trouble. Happily, it was a fairly easy job and what a difference it made.

Then we stared at a bare wall and decided we must have a fireplace. So we found two marvelous local workers to put one in. We said Richard's *Nutcracker* salary for that year helped pay for it. We have never regretted the choice.

The house was deceptive in size, having a living room with a dining area, two bedrooms, bathroom, kitchen, a large attic and basement, as well as a front lawn and back garden. Decorating a new home was fun, even though we had to be frugal.

This was a hectic year. I did a lot of painting and had enough new works to warrant another exhibition, which was held in our studio on November 12th. It was a success and very rewarding.

4. Guest Teaching. Dom Orejudos.

For a while once a week, I taught at a studio in Schaumburg. It was not a happy situation. After the long drive out there, I taught two classes to groups of mostly unruly and uninterested children in a room divided by a sliding panel that did not sufficiently silence the music from the other side.

At the same time, I was teaching once a week in La Grange for the ballet school of the Salt Creek Ballet, directed by Patricia Sigurdson, formerly of American Ballet Theatre. This was a different matter altogether. Despite being a long drive, it was a pleasure to teach there. Most of the students were talented, well trained and disciplined.

In 1990, Richard and I were settling into the house in Michigan and, as warmer weather was approaching, we decided to have a deck built at the back of the house. But the day before it was put up, I walked out of the back door and misjudged the step down. I tripped and hurt my foot. I had a feeling I had broken something and had to use my teaching stick to hop around—added to which we were having a couple of friends over for dinner.

The next day, back in Chicago, I saw my doctor who confirmed my suspicions and put my foot in a cast. It was a walking one, so I did not have to use crutches. Teaching wasn't easy, but most of our students understood hand explanations of the movements.

It was more difficult a few weeks later. I had agreed to teach at Audre Mendel's dance seminar in the Mendel Center in Benton Harbor. Her husband Herb had given major funding for the building. I hated to renege. So with the help of a good dancer to demonstrate my explanations, all went well, even the character class. I used lots of *port de bras* and *épaulment* while sitting in the chair with my foot supported by another.

News reached us that Dom Orejudos had AIDS, and it was a very sad day when we heard he died at his home in Boulder, Colorado. What a waste of talent. He had been so loyal to us, even after the closing of Illinois Ballet. He had been so much a part of it from the very beginning that, after a few years, we made him associate director.

Dom not only choreographed but designed the costumes for his own ballets, for Eric Braun's *Arabesque* production by Illinois Ballet, for our production of Ashton's *Façade* and Hy Somers *Valse Promenade*. His designs were clear, and he was always so helpful and encouraging while I tried to create what he wanted.

Dom was also a dark horse. He not only danced, choreographed and designed costumes, but he drew wonderful caricatures (we have a few), painted murals and played the violin. Then there was another side of him. He was co-owner of the Gold

Coast, a well-known gay night club, and massage parlors. He was also into the leather scene. But with us in the ballet world, which he loved, he was totally dedicated. His only regret was not being taller.

5. Margot Fonteyn. Ruth Page. Michael Somes and Wendy Ellis.

In February 1991, Johan Renvall joined us and other guests at a showing of *Desire* in our home. We still think Johan's work is the best thing in it.

On February 21ˢᵗ, while driving to Schaumburg, I heard on the radio that Margot Fonteyn died. I was so upset I should have pulled off the expressway, but I didn't. I arrived at the studio feeling awful and, to add to my misery, they were playing the "Rose Adagio" music in the adjacent room. At that point, I nearly lost it.

Why did she leave us so soon?—with the infinite knowledge and experiences she could have shared with us for many years to come.

We do have some wonderful records of her but, sadly, not of her early years on tape. Nowadays every move and thought is recorded, but I honestly think there are fewer dancers today who show an interest in her life history or that of other great dancers. Even when we were teaching, we had to keep reminding the students that they needed to read about the art they were studying. We tried to help by keeping a fairly extensive collection of ballet books at their disposal.

On March 22ⁿᵈ, we were asked to a luncheon party at Ruth Page's celebrating her birthday. Ruth was, sad to say, aging considerably. But it was still a pleasant affair, and they remembered it was also our wedding anniversary and toasted us, too.

A few days later, we were distressed to hear of Ruth's death. She had been a remarkable woman, always a charming hostess who shared stories of her fascinating life. She was so generous to us.

Two luminaries of the dance world gone in the same year. We also had our own personal loss, as dear "Steppie," as I called Daddy's Jane, passed away in August.

I was gradually completing the plans I had for a garden in Sawyer. I loved getting my hands into the earth, or dirt, as the Americans call it.

In September, our favorite "chef" Fred came to stay for a few days, and we gave a party in his honor.

I held my third watercolor exhibition in November in the studio; we were getting the set up down pat by now.

Richard celebrated his 21ˢᵗ year in *The Nutcracker*. This year, there were new sets and costumes. In our opinion, they were not as effective as the previous ones, with the exception of the "Snow Scene"—as always, one of the highlights of the production. Richard was given a handsome new costume for the first act—the design of which was displayed for a time on banners hung along downtown light poles. But for the second act, he was given an elaborate white-velvet costume. He was not happy, feeling he looked like Liberace without the candelabra. He certainly didn't look much like the

Herr Drosselmeyer of the first act. Richard let his opinions be known to the powers that be and, after a while, they agreed. He wore the first-act costume for both acts and felt much better.

The next year started badly for me. I was knocked down by a drunk outside the studio and broke my right wrist. I managed fairly well after it was put in a cast. But putting on a bra and trying to paint with my left hand were challenging. My cast came off the day before Richard's birthday. So we had a double celebration.

In March 1992, American Ballet Theatre was in town and so were Michael Somes and his wife Wendy Ellis (many people have wondered if she was our daughter). They came over from London to set Sir Fred's *Symphonic Variations* on American Ballet Theatre, and the opening was in Chicago. We didn't see much of them, but they did come to dinner one evening. Michael was funny about our apartment, saying his whole flat would have fit into our living room.

One day we found a message on our answering machine at the studio from someone asking, if I was a Houssemayne-Du Boulay, to please call Jaikie Ceisel at a certain number, which I did, and found a new cousin living in Chicago with her American husband and their two daughters. Jaikie had evidently seen my name in Richard's biography in *The Nutcracker* program. We eventually met and later her parents, Hugh and Marjorie du Boulay, came over from Scotland to visit her. After returning to Scotland, they sent me photo copies of two miniatures they own of my great, great grandparents, which I value.

In April, I was at home nursing a bad cold. While watching television, I heard about the sudden and drastic flooding of buildings in Chicago's Loop. Some buildings needed to be immediately evacuated. When Richard got home, he explained how they were told to leave the building because the elevators were going to be shut down. Richard still had to lock up the studio. By the time he finished, the elevators were already off. This meant he and two dancers had to walk down 23 floors in the dark.

For the Memorial Day weekend, we stayed with Fred and Bill in New York. We had a good time, as always, being with them.

During the summer, we realized G.T. was failing in health. He was 19 years old and suffering old-age complaints. It was heartbreaking, but we very sadly had him put to sleep. We hated the thought of taking him to the vet, so the vet came to the apartment. Richard and I left him and went for a very teary walk. He was gone when we returned to our lonely place.

Later that year, Larry Selander and his fiancée Mary Ladish came to visit us in Sawyer. We had much to talk about since Mary was from Milwaukee and had been involved with the Milwaukee Ballet. So we had many mutual friends—in particular, Basil Thompson who, after leaving the Joffrey Ballet, went to the Milwaukee Ballet first as ballet master and later as *regisseur*. Quite a few times, we drove there to see him and his wife Kitty and attend the ballet. They were good times.

Larry and Mary were married the following May in Milwaukee—a beautiful wedding, which we attended.

The weekend before Thanksgiving, I had my fourth exhibition in the studio.

6. *Gesualdo*.

In 1993 Gordon Schmidt, who had been a student of ours some years before, had been asked by Channel 11-WTTW to choreograph a section for a program to be called *Love in 4 Acts*. Three other local choreographers were to complete the hour-long television show.

After leaving us, Gordon had a varied and successful career, which included choreographing ballets for Ballet Chicago, directed by Daniel Duell and Patricia Blair.

Gordon approached us about appearing in his segment of *Love in 4 Acts*. We were delighted with the idea and agreed to do it. We would have to work around our class schedule, but Gordon was agreeable to rehearsing us in our studio—usually during our afternoon break.

His subject for *Love in 4 Acts* was the story of Gesualdo, a 16th century Italian composer who is so consumed by his work that he neglects his wife, who takes a lover. Gesualdo finds them together and kills them. He is haunted by this in his old age.

Gordon wanted Richard to portray the elder Gesualdo and for me to portray his wife. The young wife and her lover were danced by two members of Ballet Chicago, and the young Gesualdo by Olivier Munoz, a marvelous dancer from Cleveland.

We had ten rehearsals, plus costume fittings, prior to the taping. Gordon found the perfect setting in Ida Noyes Hall on the University of Chicago campus. Filming took four days. We enjoyed every moment, despite some long waits.

When the whole program was shown later, it seemed that "Gesualdo" was the most popular segment.

I was planning another exhibition of my watercolors in the studio at the beginning of November. Stanley Paul lent us an extra folding table. It was a heavy metal one, which we propped against the alley wall outside our building while Richard went to get the station wagon. But the wind knocked down the table. The edge dropped onto the back of my calf. It was an excruciating pain at first but eased off for a while. I was not happy with the look of my injury. A few days later, I went to see my doctor, who recommended therapy. During my second session, the wound started to bleed. My doctor was concerned and sent me to a vein specialist.

To my alarm, I learned that the table had almost cut to my Achilles. The specialist gave me two options: a skin graft or a lengthy treatment to be done at home daily. I did not wish for a graft, so opted for the long treatment. Though tiresome, it worked fairly well.

Chapter XII
1993-1995

1. Decision to Close School. Daniel Duell. Pianists.

We had talked briefly with Dan Duell on the subject of our studio and of the possibility of our giving up teaching in the near future. He mentioned that Ballet Chicago might be interested in taking over the studio. Dan had been asked to come to Chicago from New York, where he had been a principal dancer with the New York City Ballet, to try and save the ailing Chicago City Ballet. After its demise, he started Ballet Chicago.

Early in 1994, Dan called us and broached the subject again because he was in great need of more centralized quarters and a permanent studio.

We said we would get back to him and called Larry Selander for his opinion. We explained to him that we were seriously considering giving up the school. Besides, things were not going too well. We also had been teaching for 40 years, but the thought of just leaving a fully-equipped studio worried us. Now Dan's proposal of taking over the studio seemed the ideal solution. It meant we would not have to close the door on an empty ballet studio.

So with Larry's unending help, it was arranged that Ballet Chicago would take over our studio and most of its contents some time in the fall.

Thus we started our last term in the summer of 1994.

On the last day, we shared the class. Richard taught barre-work (there were quite a few wet eyes during *pliés*), and we both taught the *centre* and *allegro*.

The students had planned a farewell party, and quite a few "old girls" turned up, too. It was hard for us to believe it was all over. We knew that there was going to be a big gap in our lives, especially not seeing many of the students on a daily basis. Richard and I never had children. So we felt, in many cases, that the students were our "family." Most of the regulars have, over the years, endearingly called us Mr. and Mrs. "E."—and many still do.

We just hoped that, over the years, we had given some of them a love of ballet, its grace, beauty of line, awareness of posture, strength and discipline—all of which could be of help toward their goals in life, whether they chose to be professional dancers or not. Many of them became professional dancers and, all in all, were accepted into 31 dance companies here in the States and in Europe.

During our 40 years of teaching, we were fortunate to have many well-known dancers come to study with us, usually when a ballet or dance company was in town. To name just a few: Violette Verdy, Eleanor D'Antuono, Ivan Nagy, Bruce Marks, Toni Lander, William Carter, Patti Obey and many more. Sometimes other stage artists would come to class, such as Marilu Henner and, as previously mentioned, Audrey Hepburn and Julie Harris.

One day in 1963, while we were at 20 E. Jackson, Barbra Streisand appeared. She was performing at Mr. Kellys and was preparing for a film in which she had some dancing to do. A mutual friend suggested she come to us because she wanted to brush up a little. So she had private lessons with me for a short while. They were fun, to say the least.

Richard and I returned to the studio to collect some of our belongings. These included quite a few costumes, which we intended to store in the attic of our house in Michigan.

Some years earlier, after the demise of Illinois Ballet, the stage manager at the Athenaeum had lent us a small room upstairs in the theatre, where we were able to hang costumes and store some scenery. We should have kept a better check on that room. On one occasion, while searching for a needed costume, we discovered that some of the handsome period costumes for *The Moor of Venice* were missing, along with other items.

After that, we made room in the studio and hung as much as possible from lines on the ceilings of the dressing rooms. But when we left the studio, all had to be moved. One thing we did leave among others, such as the barres and mirrors, was our piano. If it hadn't been for our dear friend Robert Vanderschaaf, it would have died long before. Robert, a very fine concert pianist, spent quite a few years playing for ballet classes. He was able to do the same for us on occasions when we needed someone to substitute for some reason or another. We and the students loved it, for he was so sensitive to the dance. Also a very accomplished piano tuner, he volunteered to do something about our old piano which, like many studio pianos, had to suffer under many good, bad and indifferent pianists. He did wonders and kept the poor instrument working. It was then bequeathed to Ballet Chicago.

Over the years, we have had quite a few pianists play for our classes. We always had live music no matter how tight our finances were.

In the early days there was Matt, who would play something akin to a Rachmaninoff concerto for *pliés*, which would wake up any bleary-eyed student who attended the morning class. But Matt was an untrained pianist and pounded the piano to the point that strings broke. We could not afford that.

Bill Hughes played for a while, which was lucky for us. Then there were times when we had trouble finding anyone. One time in desperation we tried out a strange lady who could, it seems, only play "Glow Worm," which she adjusted to fit 2/4 or 3/4 or whatever. She didn't last long.

Much later, we had Tim and Dave—both of whom we liked very much. They were loyal and stayed with us even though they could have found better-paying work elsewhere.

Charlene was with us for years. She was a good pianist but not very inspiring. She couldn't improvise and played only from a stack of music that we eventually knew every note of. But she, too, was loyal and reliable. Meticulously neat, she took it upon herself to be the studio matron, insisting on neatness from the students in class, in the dressing rooms and the reception area. This was a big help to us, and we were grateful.

Richard and I were doing well loading up the station wagon parked outside the studio when, on the last trip, I stumbled on the edge of the curb and twisted my ankle. Having broken one before, I knew the feeling and was sure I had done it again—what an exit from the studio!

So once again I had a cast. At least I didn't have anything to do. I had just been looking forward to a few weeks off in Sawyer, enjoying walks on the beach or in the woods. It was not to be for a while.

One of our ex-students had an important position at the Hinsdale Center for the Arts and suggested I have an art exhibition there. Plans were put into motion, and it was decided that I would show my watercolors there for two weeks in November. Everyone there was very kind and provided a reception for me on the first day. I did well, selling quite a few paintings.

Earlier in the year, I was fortunate to have one of my paintings printed in an edition of *Dance Magazine*, contributed by Ann Barzel as dance editor for Chicago.

In November, Richard started rehearsing for *The Nutcracker* again. It made life easier not having to work around a class schedule.

2. Ballet Chicago.

Part of our agreement with Ballet Chicago was that Richard and I would teach two or three classes a week for the next two years in the ballet school which Dan and Patricia Blair (now his wife) had just opened, now that they had a more permanent home. We enjoyed being back in our old home.

Ballet Chicago was planning a production of *Coppélia*, and Dan asked Richard and me to appear. Rehearsals started in March. The ballet opened at the Shubert Theatre in early April 1995. Meredith Benson danced the role of Swanilda so well. I played her mother, and Richard was a doddering priest in the last act. Basil Thompson came in from Milwaukee to stage the ballet. We enjoyed seeing him and working with him.

In May, I held my seventh exhibition in the studio thanks to Dan and Patricia.

3. Visit to England. Royal Ballet. House in Michigan.

With no summer term to teach, we decided to take a trip to England. We left in early July for New York, where we spent two nights with Fred and Bill. Then we flew into Gatwick Airport since our friends, the Littleales, lived only a short distance away. We stayed with them for three days and had a good time. We used their home as a base from which we toured around some of our old haunts. Especially nostalgic for me was returning to East Grinstead after so many years. I always felt that it was my true English home. My father and mother were married there, and it was my grandparents' home, which I had visited so often when I was a child. We went along to see if their house was still there and, to my delight, it was.

East Grinstead had changed a little, but much of its old charm was still intact—even the old Tudor building that, a long time ago, had a fire. It happened while I was staying with my grandparents, and I remember well everyone telling the amazing story of how, after putting out the fire, one of the things they found was a pound of butter still unmelted.

Our next stop was to spend the night with friends in East Horsley, Surrey, who lived in a lovely thatched house with a beautiful garden at the end of which was an enclosed swimming pool.

From there we went to my aunts' house in Winchester. They had arranged for us to stay in a B&B near them.

My aunts were wonderful as always, both of them in their 90s, but both very blind. It amazed us how well they managed to get around. I pray that I have some of their longevity.

My aunt Peggy was at one time a governess working in such places as Teheran, Prague and Switzerland. She was a tutor to young children as well.

Alison was a teacher at a school in Croydon. During World War II, she was in the U.S.A. as a cipher worker. Returning to England, she joined the WVS (Women's Voluntary Service) with her friend Stella Macdonald. Stella's father had been the British Ambassador in Peking during the Boxer Rebellion. She was there at the time with her parents and, because of that, she was asked to verify details of events during the filming of *Sixty Days in Peking*. David Niven portrayed her father.

Many years ago, when I was a little girl, my aunts Alison and Peggy compiled a small book about me, my Seelyham dog and my garden. It was handwritten, hand-illustrated and put together by hand. It is a treasured possession.

While we were in Winchester we made two more stops, the first to Winchester College, where many of my male relatives had studied. One house is named after my great grandfather. We found Du Boulay House. I felt very proud. Later when Robert Irving was conducting for the Sadler's Wells Ballet, he informed me that he had attended Du Boulay House.

Our next stop was the beautiful Winchester Cathedral. The exterior is not exceptional, but the interior is awe inspiring.

From Winchester, we drove to Bournemouth and then to Salisbury where we spent the night, giving us enough time to visit the famous Cathedral. What a delight to the eye it is. Even though there was scaffolding around the spire, its proportions were perfect. Yet, strangely, the interior was not as perfect—the opposite to Winchester Cathedral.

Bath was our next destination. Richard had been there before when touring with the ballet, but it was my first visit. It was just as wonderful as I had been told. We walked a lot and took a tour bus, feeling this is always the best way to see a place when one has only a limited time there.

It was fun to be in the original Pump Room, as opposed to the one in Chicago in the Ambassador Hotel, where Stanley Paul appeared for so many years. We sent him a card saying he should play here, too.

From Bath, we drove to London and stayed with our friends Michael and Ann.

Before we left America, Audre Mendel had given us explicit instructions to visit the reconstruction of the Globe Theatre on the South Bank of the Thames. She and her husband were major contributors to the project. Sam Wanamaker, who started it, had been a good friend of theirs.

Audre gave us the name of a lady who would give us a guided tour of the building. It was a clear, sunny day and London looked magnificent. The view across the river of St. Paul's Cathedral was so impressive. Wearing hard hats, we took a most informative tour of the theatre still being constructed.

It was also good to have a chance to see our dear friends, Moira Tucker and Leslie Edwards.

Leslie arranged for us to watch a Royal Ballet rehearsal at Talgarth Gardens. It was for *Daphnis and Chloë*, one of my favorites. I had been in the premiere, and it brought back many memories.

At the rehearsal we saw Christopher Newton, who asked if we would like to see the company at the Opera House that evening. They were performing *Giselle*. We were thrilled and sat in staff seats with Monica Mason and Donald MacLeary.

During the times when we returned to London, we tried to visit the Royal Ballet whenever possible. But our holiday time often coincided with the time when the company was not there.

We did get to the Royal Ballet School, both at Talgarth Gardens and White Lodge, on a few visits. When we did go to the company performances, we had the pleasure of seeing some works that were new to us: Ashton's *Sylvia, Enigma Variations*, a gem, and *Ondine*, created especially for Fonteyn.

We saw an early ballet by Kenneth MacMillan, *The Invitation*, with a memorable performance by Lynn Seymour; also MacMillan's *Elite Syncopations, The Prince of the Pagodas* and *Gloria*.

One time, when we were given our complimentary tickets, we found that our seats were in the staff box (where de Valois sat so often watching our performances.) John Cranko's *The Lady and the Fool* was on the program. Another time, we saw John's *Pineapple Poll*, a delightful piece. Of the classics, we saw Fokine's *Firebird* and *Petrouchka*. When the company came to Chicago, we were able to see ballets that were new to us: Ashton's *La Fille Mal Guardée, The Dream* and *Monotones I and II*; and MacMillan's *Mayerling* and *Romeo and Juliet*.

I regret not continuing to keep my list of ballets and companies that I have seen, as I did in England. But once I became a professional dancer and was in so many ballets myself, where I used to notate having seen *Le Lac des Cygnes* or *Les Sylphides* by a stroke on the page, the strokes went off the page. So I gave up in the end. Before that time, I had seen 20 different ballet companies.

One day, Ann Morley drove us around Anerley to some of Richard's old haunts, like the building he lived in, the one where his first ballet classes were held and the wine ship that belonged to his grandfather. It was still a wine shop, so Richard went in and the new owners let him look around and go down to the basement, where he had been many times before. Ann then took us to the Crystal Palace grounds. The Palace itself was long gone, but the grounds were still fairly intact. Richard saw the dirt track course, where he used to ride, and the famous replicas of dinosaurs that he had described to me in detail. They certainly were impressive.

Then we flew back to Chicago.

Because our house in Sawyer had no garage, we parked our car outside. Many evergreens hung over our driveway and dropped sap onto our car. It was fiendish to get off. So Richard built a carport. No more sap.

We love our little house and its proximity to Lake Michigan. We have always wanted to live near water, maybe because water was never far away in London. A leisurely half-hour walk down our road takes us to the lake shore. The beach is wide and sandy, and sometimes there is not a soul to be seen. Peace. Being on the eastern shore of the lake, we see the most spectacular sunsets.

Going away from the lake, we can find blueberry patches, vineyards, orchards, cornfields, old farmyards and their barns, beautiful woods, flat lands, rolling hills and all the seasons. The glorious autumnal coloring is enhanced by the contrast of the evergreens. Then comes the excitement of spring after the only bad thing: the harsh winters. But our house is cozy, especially when we are sitting in front of our wood-burning fire. Even if it snows and the next day the sky is a clear bright blue, it is a wonderful sight. All of this inspires me as I try to capture some of it in watercolors.

Ironically in August, our dear friend Ted—who was one of our main reasons for coming to Sawyer—had decided, for financial reasons, to leave Sawyer and live with his family in Denver. We hated to see him go and missed him so much.

4. Ruth Page Awards. Richard's 25th Year in *The Nutcracker*.

The Ruth Page Awards Committee informed us that we were to receive the Lifetime Service to the Field Award. It was nice to be remembered and so honored. The awards dinner and reception were given on September 10th. Gordon Schmidt gave a delightful introductory speech, and many of our friends, colleagues and ex-students were there, adding to the pleasure of the event.

In 1995, Richard celebrated his 25th year in the role of Herr Drosselmeyer in Ruth's *The Nutcracker*. He never missed a single performance in all that time. Everybody admired his portrayal, and many of the dancers were fascinated with his make-up.

Some would come and watch him applying his make-up—an art in itself. The Sadler's Wells repertoire had very few abstract ballets in it, favoring the classics and storytelling ballets, which required us to make up for a variety of characters. We always did our own make-up but were so fortunate to be in the company of artists who helped us carry on this fascinating tradition.

To celebrate the 25 years, Larry and Mary planned a surprise party for Richard in their beautiful home. It was a festive occasion, and a complete surprise for Richard who thought we were going there for dinner. Instead, he found the dining room lined with friends and ex-students. He was stunned and delighted.

Chapter XIII
The Gala

1. Invitation to Attend Gala at The Royal Opera House

In December, 1995 we received an unexpected letter from Sir Anthony Dowell, director of the Royal Ballet, saying there was to be a celebration of the 50th anniversary of the reopening of the Royal Opera House after World War II, on February 20th, 1996. They would mark the occasion with a performance of *The Sleeping Beauty* as the Sadler's Wells did in 1946. Anthony was inviting as many of the original cast as was possible to appear in a *défilé* at the beginning of the last act. He hoped we would be able to join the company, and he looked forward to hearing from us.

Richard and I were thrilled at the prospect and said, even if we had to row, we would get there.

2. London. Diaghilev Exhibition.

1996 started with us making plans for our trip to London for the Gala in February. We no longer had friends or family who could put us up, except Michael and Ann who were going to be away for part of the time. So we wrote to Leslie Edwards and asked him for help. We heard from him soon to say that Wendy Ellis, Michael Somes' widow, said we could stay in her flat since she was going to be away then. It was welcome news, and we immediately wrote to her and made definite plans.

On arriving in London, Michael Jervis drove us to Wendy's flat near the Sadler's Wells Theatre.

Because we arrived a few days prior to the Gala, we had time to see a few friends, including a delightful dinner with my cousin Jane at her house with some of her artist friends. Added to our delight, we found a Diaghilev exhibition was being held at the Barbican Art Gallery. It was marvelous. Most of the works, many never seen here before, were from Russia. They included costume designs (I particularly relished the Leon Bakst ones in watercolor), original costumes in surprisingly good condition, posters, photographs and set cloths. We also watched a documentary film shown on Diaghilev, his life and his works. We were very lucky to have experienced this remarkable collection, as we learned it was not going to be shown anywhere else in the West.

Seeing this exhibition reinforced my feelings about what is involved to create a satisfying dance program. Perhaps because I am such a purist, I get a little tired of bare stages, where the only scenic designer is the lighting designer. I fully understand that there are economic reasons for much of this, but it is such a joy to see a ballet where all the major elements blend successfully: the dance, the music and the scenic art.

Also, I feel that nowadays there is too much emphasis on athleticism. Incredible as are some of the movements the dancers have to perform, there is little depth of character. I long to see more real people performing and not what appear, in many instances, to be automatons. Added to this, there is so much intensity. I want to go to the theatre to get away from everyday problems and enter into a world that is more uplifting and full of beauty to the eyes and ears, as ballet can be.

3. Royal Opera House. Queen Elizabeth II.

On the morning of the Gala, we arrived at the main entrance of the Opera House and were greeted by Sir Anthony Dowell. He directed us to the pit lobby, where the old members were to gather. There were quite a few there already. There was much hugging and kissing and delight at seeing friends after so long. There was also a feeling of sadness at knowing that Margot, Fred and Bobby were no longer with us.

There was a little shock, too. We hardly recognized a few people, especially Violetta Elvin, once a raven-haired beauty now a bright blonde. Julia Farron, Beryl Grey, Rosemary Lindsay and Gillian Lynne, to name a few, looked so well. After much talk over coffee, we were all called to the stage for our rehearsal with the company. Little did we think we would ever tread those boards again. It really was a thrill. We were asked to line up in alphabetical order. Because, professionally, I used to spell my name with a small d, I was considered a B, and so was third in line. Then we were divided into two groups, one on either side of the stage.

To the march from the opening of the third act of *The Sleeping Beauty*, we were told to walk one at a time down a few steps from a dais, which was part of the set upstage center, then to walk downstage, where a student from the Royal Ballet School would present the ladies with a bouquet of flowers and the men with a bottle of champagne. After accepting these, we were to curtsy or bow to Her Majesty the Queen, who would be in the Royal Box on stage left, then walk off stage, line up, before walking on to stand beside chairs that had been placed along the wings, where we were to sit during Act III.

At the beginning of the Apotheosis, we were instructed to get up and walk in file back to the dais and stand until the end of the act.

After the rehearsal, we were given our theatre tickets and passes to two gatherings to be held during the evening in the famous Crush Bar. We found we had been given an extra ticket for a friend. So we hastily called my cousin Jane, knowing she had been longing to go to the performance but had been unable to get a seat.

Richard and I went back to the flat to spruce up in our formal wear.

Cabbing it back to the Opera House, we met Jane in the lobby and took our seats in the second row of the main floor, with an excellent view of the Royal Box. There was an air of expectancy. The orchestra was in the pit; the conductor was at the podium; the house was full; and most of the audience was in formal attire—an elegant array. We looked around at the familiar surroundings of the beautiful auditorium; the wonderful warm red-plush seats; the red-striped wall coverings; the delicate pink shades for the lights which, in groups of three, were around the famous horseshoe dress circle and boxes; and the magnificent front of the stage curtains, with their huge embossed Royal Coat-of-Arms.

After the entrance of Her Majesty and her niece, Lady Sara Snowdon (Princess Margaret's daughter), and the playing of the National Anthem, we watched the Prologue and Act I of *The Sleeping Beauty*. We were not impressed with the new sets and costumes. The overpowering sets seemed to diminish the dancers, who were overdressed in fussy costumes that did not enhance their line. We longed for the beautiful Oliver Messel designs. Darcy Bussell was a lovely Aurora, but we couldn't help but remember Margot and Bobby and Fred, who had been marvelous as Carabosse.

Between the Prologue and Act I, there was a reception in the Crush Bar. Madam was there in a wheelchair, looking wonderful for her 97 years.

After the first act, we had to go backstage to prepare for our *grand défilé*.

Even though there were TVs in the dressing rooms so we could watch the second act, we were all too busy catching up on news with each other that we didn't see much of it.

Then we were called to the stage and nervously waited in the wings. We were concerned about timing our moves correctly to the musical counts allotted to each of us. If we made a mistake on our walk downstage, our names would be out of order while Anthony announced us to the audience. All went well. I received a beautiful bouquet of flowers, curtsied to the Queen and walked offstage. Richard was about four or five after me and, after receiving his bottle of Moët Chandon, gave a classical ballet bow to her Majesty. He said it felt more appropriate for the occasion.

It was exciting to be on stage for all of the last act and, fortunately, Richard and I were sitting on stage right—giving us a perfect view of the Royal Box. Then Madam was wheeled into the downstage wing by the proscenium, where she sat for the last act. I was lucky to be only one seat away from her and therefore able to hear her comments and watch her reactions to the dancers.

When all we "old ones" reached our places on the dais and the act was over, the curtain was lowered and they wheeled a table onto center stage. On it was a huge cake, with "50th Anniversary" written on it.

The curtain was raised again, with the audience still in its seats and the house lights on—a majestic sight.

Angus Sterling, chairman of the Royal Opera House, welcomed Dame Ninette, who made her entrance with the aid of a walker to thunderous applause and a standing ovation—more emotion on my part.

Angus Sterling gave a short speech thanking the Queen and praising Dame Ninette, who then cut the cake. Finally the curtain was lowered, and we were asked to remain onstage—whereupon Anthony arranged us and the principal dancers into two half-circles. We all applauded as Her Majesty came onstage followed by

John Major, the Prime Minister. Anthony introduced the Queen to all the dancers and to each of us, who in turn either curtsied or bowed as Her Majesty offered her gloved hand.

On introducing me, Anthony explained that I had come from the States for this occasion. One is not supposed to speak to the Queen unless spoken to, but I blurted out, "I'm sorry Ma'am, but I'm afraid I am a defector." I feared she might say, "Send her to the Tower—off with her head!" But she only smiled and moved on, much to my relief.

After Her Majesty's exit, we made our way to the Crush Bar again, and crush it was. But there was wonderful food and drinks and many people to see.

Then it was finally time to leave and come back to reality. It was surely a once-in-a-lifetime event.

We have framed the program from this gala, and it hangs in our hallway beside another frame that contains the program from the 1939 gala. One shows the first time Richard and I were on the Royal Opera House stage together, and the other the last time. Also, it was at the Opera House where we first met. So it was especially momentous that, after 49 years of marriage, we were able to enjoy this last great occasion together.

How blessed we have been.

Epilogue

As of this date, it has been 54 years since Richard and I made the leap across the Atlantic after leaving the Sadler's Wells Ballet.

Thirty-five years have passed since the Illinois Ballet's last performance and 12 years since we closed our school. Nine years ago Ruth Page's *The Nutcracker* closed, and Richard gave his final performance as Herr Drosselmeyer.

I have reason to believe that Richard is the sole living male dancer of the Vic-Wells Ballet from its 1933 season.

I have given only fleeting glimpses of the celebrated artists with whom we have so fortunately been associated. Much has been written about them already. Therefore I hope, if the readers are interested in learning more, they will research the material available. It is fascinating and part of the history of ballet.

July 2006

Biographies

CHRISTINE DU BOULAY was born in London, England. Following her scholastic training, she studied at the Central School of Art and at the Sadler's Wells School of Ballet.

Her first professional engagement was with England's International Ballet. Subsequently, she was asked to join the Sadler's Wells Ballet for its first performance at the re-opening of the Royal Opera House after World War II, where she met Richard Ellis.

They were married and were on the first two tours of the United States and Canada—after which time they came to live in Chicago, where they directed and taught at the Ellis-Du Boulay School of Ballet.

Christine also co-directed the Illinois Ballet, for which she made all the costumes. She appeared in one of the many television programs that the company performed in on WTTW-Channel 11, Chicago's Public Broadcasting Station, and also in a segment of "Love in 4 Acts" on the same station.

Now enjoying retirement, Christine has returned to her old love: watercolors. She has had many successful exhibitions.

RICHARD ELLIS, a native of London, England, was a child actor and dancer, joining the Vic-Wells Ballet in 1933. In 1940, he joined the Royal Navy, commanding a flotilla of landing craft on D-Day. After the war, he returned to the Sadler's Wells Ballet for its first season at the Royal Opera House, where he met Christine Du Boulay, who became his wife a year later.

After the first two tours of America, deciding to immigrate to Chicago, they opened their own school of ballet, where they taught for 40 years. During this time, they created and directed the Illinois Ballet for 12 years, performing extensively in Chicago and neighboring states and on WTTW-Channel 11.

Richard staged Sir Frederick Ashton's *Façade* for the Joffrey, Houston and Ruth Page's ballet companies. For 27 years, he appeared as Herr Drosselmeyer in Ruth Page's annual production of *The Nutcracker*.

LUCIA MAURO, editor, studied at the Ellis-Du Boulay School of Ballet, where she was inspired to pursue a career as a dance critic and arts writer. The Ellises, through their dedication to dance and nurturing teaching style, have served as significant role models in her life. Lucia's work appears in the *Chicago Tribune, Chicago Magazine, The Chicago Collection* and several national arts publications, such as *Dance Magazine, Dance Teacher, Dance Spirit* and *Stage Directions*. She is the dance contributor for WBEZ-Chicago Public Radio's "848" program and is featured on "The Chicago Dance Project," a series that aired on WTTW-Channel 11. Lucia is the author of three books for McGraw-Hill, including *Careers for the Stagestruck & Other Dramatic Types*, and hosts the popular "About Dance" program at the Chicago Cultural Center and the Auditorium Theatre's FireSide Chats.